WISDOM

How to Be Alive, Rich, and Free

Other Books by Sid Huston

BASK: Real Spirituality

BASK: Sexual Freedom

BASK: Unsinkable

BASK: Satisfaction

BASK: Comfort

BASK: Glory!

BASK: Abundance (future title)

BASK WISDOM

How to Be Alive, Rich, and Free

By Sid Huston

The BASK Series of Christian Fiction

Copyright © 2017 by Sid Huston
Colorado Springs, CO
All Rights Reserved.

Please visit our website at www.BASK.Love.

No part of this book may be reproduced or transmitted in any form or by any means, electronic or mechanical, including photocopying, recording, or by any information storage and retrieval system without the written permission of the publisher, except where permitted by law or for brief quotations for the purpose of printed reviews. Please direct all inquiries to Sidhuston@msn.com.

Printed in the United States

Songs are in the public domain, written by Sid Huston, or excerpted with permission.

BASK: Wisdom is a work of fiction placed in a historical context. Where real-life historical figures appear, the situation, incidents, locales, and dialogues concerning those persons are entirely fictional and are not intended to depict actual events. In all other respects, any resemblance to actual persons, living or dead, events or locales is entirely coincidental.

This book is not intended as a substitute for the medical advice of physicians, therapists or other medical and mental health professionals.

In addition, this book is designed to provide information and motivation to the reader. The publisher and author are not engaged to render any type of psychological, legal, or any other kind of professional advice. No warranties and guarantee are expressed or implied by the author.

ISBN: 978-0-9992107-0-3
eISBN: 978-0-9992107-1-0

Dedication

I have sailed and I have captured a treasure trove of valuable insights that I want to give to you. These precious gems are the rare wisdom principles that can make you truly rich.

Some of the fellows I have sailed with have been a tremendous help to me. Others were *picaroons and miscreants* and I have learned from their mischief. The best were real CROWN wearing champions for Christ and they took me under their wing. I have been made rich by these experiences.

I know that faith in God, commitment to family, and real love is what really matters in this life. This book will help you acquire these riches. You can have all of this when you learn to walk in wisdom!

I dedicate this book to Aiden and Ean with the hope that they would soon come to know God personally. I also hope that they will walk with the wise and grow wise!

The great poet Henry Wadsworth Longfellow said in 'A Psalm of Life':

> *Lives of great men all remind us*
> *We can make our lives sublime,*
> *And, departing, leave behind us*
> *Footprints in the sands of time.*
>
> *Footprints, that perhaps another,*
> *Sailing O'er life's solemn Main,*
> *A forlorn and shipwrecked brother,*
> *Seeing, shall take heart again.*

I wrote this to inspire you to believe and to live boldly. Wisdom is not mere knowledge, and it is not just the knowledge of God and His precious Word applied to our lives, it is a personal relationship with Wisdom Incarnate. He alone is the source of the abundant life. Live under the spout where the glory comes out! Bask in His sunshine and enjoy freedom in the current of His grace.

I hope this little book makes you feel sand in your toes and gets you to splash around in the seas. I love you and want you to know:

But of Him you are in Christ Jesus, who became for us wisdom from God—and righteousness and sanctification and redemption— ³¹ that, as it is written, "He who glories, let him glory in the LORD. (1 Corinthians 1:30-31)."

Love life and see good days. Godspeed and *Sail on!*

Sid Huston

Table of Contents

Dedication v
Preface ix
What Is BASK? xi
Introduction... xv
Pirate Speak xxi

1. Bringing In the Sheaves.................................... 1
2. Beware of Pirates 19
3. The "Real" Pearl Story.................................... 35
4. The Hummingbird 51
5. Earl's "Broken" Horses 71
6. Pirates Are Liars, Perverted, and Bound 87
7. Prudence, Understanding, and Sensibility......... 107
8. Courage to Love and Marry............................. 127
9. Be Winsome and Generous 147
10. Live, "Fully Alive" (Enthusiasm) 157
11. Loose Lips Sink Ships..................................... 177
12. BASK in the Story... 199

Songs and Authors 217
Scripture Index... 219
About the Author 223

Special Feature: The end of each chapter contrasts Real Gold Nuggets of Wisdom to pyrite (Fool's Gold).

Preface

Ahoy, matey. When people ask me what I do, and I tell them that I write pirate books to teach spiritual truth, they respond with a hearty, "Wow!"

This idea has attracted lots of interest because it relates to the spiritual life so well. We all have a little pirate in us that is trying to persuade us to run the *Jolly Roger* up the mast and begin to *chase* something inappropriate.

I live to help people discover freedom by appropriating the power of a true identity. As you read on, you will see how this passion comes through in these colorful stories. People *go on account* (become pirates) because they think a pirate life is full of adventure, and it will make them alive, rich, and free.

If you really want to be fully alive, rich, and free, you will want to read on, because it takes true wisdom to get you into the current of spiritual prosperity. This BASK.Love series of Christian fiction books will show you how to let light, life, and love into your life. *Avast*, see yourself in these exciting stories and *sail on!*

What Is BASK?

Bask: To be in the sunshine, to enjoy the situation, to relax, to lie in glory. Synonyms: To delight in, derive pleasure, enjoy, savor, comfort, and rollick.

The author's take on BASK:

Bless: Bless the LORD with your soul (mind, will, and emotions).

1
Bless the LORD, O my soul;
And all that is within me, *bless* His holy name!
2
Bless the LORD, O my soul,
And forget not all His benefits:
3
Who forgives all your iniquities,
Who heals all your diseases,
4
Who redeems your life from destruction,
Who crowns you with lovingkindness
and tender mercies.
(Psalm 103:1–4)

Ask: Ask Him for what you need. (A pirate meets his needs in his own way; the believer trusts God to meet his or her needs.)

24
"Until now you have asked nothing in My name. Ask, and you will receive, that your joy may be full."
(John 16:24)

Stay: Stay Believing, Stay Abiding, Stay Steadfast.

57
But thanks *be* to God, who gives us the victory through our Lord Jesus Christ.
58
Therefore, my beloved brethren, be steadfast, immovable, always abounding in the work of the Lord, knowing that your labor is not in vain in the Lord.
(1 Corinthians 15:57–58)

5
"I am the vine, you *are* the branches. He who abides in Me, and I in him, bears much fruit; for without Me you can do nothing."
(John 15:5)

Know: That God is for you! Know the assurance of your salvation and the assurance of answered prayer:

11
And this is the testimony: that God has given us eternal life, and this life is in His Son.

12
He who has the Son has life; he who does not have the Son of God does not have life.
13
These things I have written to you who believe in the name of the Son of God, that you may know that you have eternal life, and that you may *continue to* believe in the name of the Son of God.
(1 John 5:11–13)

Confidence and Compassion in Prayer:

14
Now this is the confidence that we have in Him, that if we ask anything according to His will, He hears us.
15
And if we know that He hears us, whatever we ask, we know that we have the petitions that we have asked of Him.
(1 John 5:14–15)

This is what it means to "BASK." We bask in the Lord, and we delight in His glory and presence!

Bless, Ask, Stay, Know! Bask. This is the way to be truly Alive, Free, and Rich!

Introduction
The BASK Series of Christian Fiction
WISDOM

Pirates will chase anything at the drop of a tricorne hat, except wisdom. This story about "Red-Legs" Greaves was much too rich to be *marooned*. Like most people who struggle with some form of bondage, Red grew up as a child of slaves. His slavery was forced upon him because his parents were Scottish conscripts. Born in Barbados, his parents were tried for treason and sold by England's first Lord Protector Oliver Cromwell, also known as "Old Ironsides." He was in charge of the Commonwealth of England, Scotland, and Ireland. As the story goes, Red's father was on the wrong team during the English Civil War. When Cromwell came into the position of power, many of the Scottish and Irish warriors were rounded up and sentenced to serve as grunt labor on English ships.

Red had a rough start in life. He came into the world as a slave from birth. His life was brutal; he went from one beating to another, from one rejection to another, from one bad master to another. Several times he swam to safety only to discover that he had gone from bad to worse. He discovered that pirates were terrible sea captains, as they were self-protecting reprobates.

From an early age, Red was orphaned; yet his life didn't end like most pirates with an early brutal death. Red was able to enjoy a long and fruitful life. Something happened to him that changed the course of his life. This treatise of historical fiction begins with Red being in the Port Royal Jail on June 7, 1692, just before noon. Having been betrayed by a former pirate comrade, Red was now waiting for his punishment. As a pirate, he was going to receive his due. It is true. He had been a pirate; the evidence was against him, and he would be hung or *gibbeted*. While sitting in his jail cell contemplating his demise, Red felt a massive jolt and heard a loud thud and horrific screams. Before he could say; "*shiver me timbers*," the jailhouse broke. It crashed into the sea, and Red was quickly washed out into the bay, treading water. Sighting a whaling ship at the inlet, Red was able to swim to safety, or so he thought.

This is where this *Wisdom* book begins. Wisdom enters into this story and helps Red make decisions that will bring him into an abundant life. This book draws on the wisdom of King Solomon from the Book of Proverbs and shows Red and the reader how to discover life, freedom, and true riches. Soon you will see that wisdom naturally flows out of your vibrant relationship with the only wise God. Certainly, you will be growing in knowledge and insights to your life situations. This book has a unique feature at the end of each chapter as it contrasts the "Gold Nuggets" of wisdom to "Fool's Gold." Just like the cheap mineral pyrite that glitters and grabs your attention, fools gold brings no real value to your life. There is a lot of fake stuff pirates will try to *hornswaggle* you with. So, take some time and *avast* the differences. If you do this, you are sure to grow in wisdom. Learn as Red does—that when you walk with the wise—you will grow wise.

Pirates have no idea that wisdom is a true treasure and extremely valuable. It is valuable because it can make the possessor truly alive, rich and free. Wisdom doesn't come into port via the trade winds; it is a gift God wants to give to all of His children, and He makes it available to all who want it. This book will serve as a treasure map showing you how to locate this valuable commodity and it will also show you how to apply wisdom to your everyday situations.

There is a treasure trove of valuable wisdom in this book. It will show you how to have good relationships and how to avoid the bad. It will show you how to acquire the discipline needed for lasting success. This read will even show you how to make good investments with your life. It will show you how to avoid trouble and how to make good choices. This book even contains secret knowledge about how to discover love, joy, and peace: true treasure that money cannot purchase; treasure that must be applied to one's own life. All in all, if you really want to find satisfaction in life, this book will be a valuable experience for you.

This book is part of the BASK series of Christian Fiction and contains the exciting real-life stories of Captain Henry Morgan and 'Red Legs' Greaves. Throughout the series, you will be challenged by the adventures of Calico Jack Rackham, Anne Bonne and Mary Reed. Their thievery explains piracy to the bone. The life-giving treasure of this series is discovered by a little Christian community that was spared from the devastating earthquake and learned to live life to the full on the remaining sand sliver of Port Royal Jamaica. This small community would later move to Spanish Town where this Wisdom story unfolds.

This series revolves around colorful characters like Tim who was just a teen when he was shanghaied from the Port of London. He survived a brutal pirate ship experience and thanks to an old sea dog named Chase he was able to arrive in Port Royal Jamaica alive. While in Port Royal he meets up with Papa Peter who was a former Franciscan Christian missionary who helps Tim discover true and life-giving treasure from the Holy Scriptures. Peter also has a beautiful daughter named Esther, and a delightful love story ensues.

This BASK.Love series of Christian fiction is entertaining, but it is also spiritually enriching. As you dive into *Wisdom*, you will discover what really has value in this life and how to attain it. As you learn to walk with wisdom, you will soon discover the truth that enables you to be truly alive, rich, and free. *Sail on!*

(BASK.Love is a website where you will discover more spiritual enriching treasure. More stories and more inspiration for you to claim.)

Pirate Speak

Insights that will help you break the pirate code!

Addled: to be mad or insane, maybe just plain stupid
Ahoy: hello
Avast: hold fast, stop and pay attention
Aye: a pirate way of saying yes; but ye never really know if he means it
Begad: by God!
Bilge: the lowest part of the ship inside the hull along the keel, thus nonsense or foolish talk—how low can you go?
Bilge-sucking: uncomplimentary expression
Blaggard: an insult
Blouse: a loose-fitting shirt
Booty: loot
Boucan-knife: a quick-strike weapon used to hack and slash to overpower others, kept hidden under the blouse
Buccaneer: Caribbean pirates
Bucko: used as "me bucko," "my friend"
Bunghole: Food was stored in wooden casks, and the stopper in the barrel was called the bung. Pirate

food was bad, so being called a bunghole wasn't a compliment.

C or Si: a Spanish pirate term for "yes!"

Cap'n: short for Captain

Cat-o'-nine-tails: or cat, for whip made of nine leather straps used for flogging; it will smarten you up!

Chase: ship being pursued

Cockswain: the Cap'n's attendant, one who would do the rowing

Corsair: a romantic term for Pirate

Crow's Nest: the platform near the top of the mast, a position for a lookout

Cutlass: a curved sword

Cutter: a single mast sailing vessel that is rigged fore and aft with two or more head sails

Dance the Hempen Jig: to hang from a noose made of hemp

Davy Jones's Locker: the bottom of the sea

Dead Men Tell No Tales: A dead man cannot betray you with their secrets; therefore a pirate would much rather turn them into sharkbait so that they could not bite them back by telling something incriminating.

Doldrums: Your ship is on the sea with no wind in your sails. A time of inactivity and stagnation, life is dull, listless, and the crew is depressed. When sailing men are in the doldrums, you just never know what stupid things they will do.

Doubloon: a Spanish gold coin

Feed the Fish: when you are thrown overboard

Freebooter: a pirate, one who seeks to live free by plundering others

Gang Plank: *a removable footway between the ship and the pier, also known as the gang way*
Gangway: *"Get out of my way."*
Go on Account: *to become a pirate*
Godspeed: *good-bye and good luck*
Grog: *an alcoholic drink; pirates prefer rum*
Hornswaggle: *to cheat or defraud; to act like a pirate*
I or Aye: *"Yes"*
Jolly Roger: *the Pirates' skull and crossbones flag, an invitation to surrender*
Kiss the Gunner's Daughter: *punishment; to be bent over a cannon and flogged*
Lad, Lass, Lassie: *someone younger than you (lass and lassie are females)*
Land Ho: *a sailor's cry to announce the sight of land, and a way to say "watch out, rum, here I come."*
Landlubber: *"lubber," an old English term for being big, slow, clumsy, not very skilled, as if they said, "I bet you were no better on land."*
Letters of Marque: *papers used by a national government entitling a private seagoing vessel to raid enemy commerce*
Maroon: *to be abandoned and deserted; a convenient way for pirates to get rid of someone without actually killing him*
Matey: *a cheerful and friendly pirate address*
Me Hearties: *a way a Cap'n would address his crew*
On the Account: *to go from being a government worker (privateer) to a pirate*
Picaroon: *a Spanish term of derision meaning a rascal*

Piece of Eight: a Spanish silver coin that could be cut into eight pieces
Pillage: to raid, rob, and sack
Pirate: a seagoing robber and murderer
Port: a seaport
Privateer: an armed private ship authorized by a country's government with Letters of Marque to attack foreign ships. Often their goal was to capture foreign ships rather than sink them. They were paid to raid, and then they would divide the loot with their sponsoring government, the investors, and the crew.
R or Arrrr: glee
Rum: a traditional pirate drink
Sail Ho!: "I see a ship."
Scuppers: spaces on the deck edge which allow water to drain back into the sea
Scurvy: a disease caused by the lack of vitamin C; a bad sickness, and a derogatory term, "ye scurvy dogs"
Sea Dog: a very experienced sailor, one with lots of stories to tell, stories that always get bigger and better with time
Sharkbait: Your foes are about to feed the fish, or a worthless and lazy sailor, a "lubber."
Shiver Me Timbers: shock or disbelief, perhaps from the shock of running the ship into a reef or from being hit with a cannon ball
Shipshape: a well-organized ship, under control, finished or complete
Sink Me: surprise
Splicing the Main Brace: After a strong storm or a fierce sea battle, when the main brace that held the

main sail was broken, it would have to be repaired. It would have to be spliced together with another pole. This was dangerous work, ropes would have to be held steady, and hemp rope would be used to wrap or splice the brace. The man in charge would reward this effort by giving his sailors an extra ration of rum. Today this phrase is a euphemism for "let's go get drunk."

Swashbuckling: *having the exciting manner or behavior of pirates, especially those depicted in films (obsolete,* **swash** *to make the noise of a sword striking a shield +* **buckler** *[shield])*

Walking the Plank: *a severe form of punishment where someone would be forced to walk a long and narrow piece of wood (a plank) off the boat and end up making a splash in the cold wet water, alone. AKA "sharkbait."*

Yo-ho-ho: *a pirate thing to say*

1.

Bringing In the Sheaves

*T*errorists have a way of getting what they want. Francesco had been taken prisoner and could have had his head lopped off, because that is what the Prophet Mohammad instructed his jihadists to do. His aim was to take civilization back to the seventh century and bring the world into submission to Islam. This is what *Islam* means. Francesco thought he would make his "earthly" father proud by going to war and resisting these barbarians. However, now he is sure that his father is angry at him, the world, and his religion.

When these terrorists discovered that Francesco's father was a wealthy silk and cloth merchant, they acted like pirates and held Francesco for ransom. They used him as collateral and trade bait to acquire the *loot* they wanted to fund their conquests. For the better part of a year, their emissaries negotiated with Pietro Di

Bernardone outside Assisi, Italy. Pietro was conflicted to the core of his being because money meant more to him than love. Eventually a price was reached, a ransom was paid, and Francesco returned home in poor shape. He had been brutalized and was in need of repair physically, emotionally, and spiritually.

Pietro believed he had been *hornswoggled* because his son was just a shell of a man and would be bedridden for a good while. When Francesco came to his senses and his strength was restored, he had no interest in dyeing cloth or in trading silks. His father was furious and sure his son had gone mad. Francis began to act differently, though not indifferent. He began to enjoy the bird on the windowsill and he gloried in its singing. He loved how it worshiped God with its beautiful voice and flew in freedom.

Francis, as he would later be called, began to talk with God in a conversational and intimately personal way. He reckoned that the God who made the vast and infinite universe was also just as intimate and concerned for him. He thought God is both infinite and intimate and understood that the God who clothed the lilies of the fields and fed the birds of the air had him and each of us in His "much-more" care.

While on his sickbed, light entered his soul and his body, and his human spirit came alive as he believed this truth. Francis began to explore the idea of knowing God personally. As he directed his thoughts heavenward, his mind was renewed. Inspired by Scriptures he had learned as a boy, he made little worshipful songs and sang to God. While he did this, his countenance lifted and he felt free. He was visited by that encouraging bird; it caught his attention and taught him a spiritual lesson. It flew into his bedroom window and lit on his bed. When it flew out, Francis opened his window and walked out on the roof tiles, where it came to him and fluttered up into his cupped hand. Francis knew something beautiful had happened in his spirit, and he determined to let this light, life, and love have him for the rest of his life.

The people who observed this irrational behavior thought he was demented and were leery of him—and so was his earthly father. As Francis was being revived, his only aspiration was to love God and serve poor people. Pietro became furious because he believed if a person couldn't afford to buy his silks, they were not worth his time or his sons' time. Realizing that he would never be able to please his earthly father, Francis devoted himself to pleasing and delighting in his Heavenly Father.

He spent more time at the cathedral and became disenchanted because of the impersonal nature of the services and the dead orthodoxy he witnessed. He found that the religious rituals made God seem far away, and this wasn't aligned with his experience or his belief. In time he was able to understand the situation, and with simple wisdom he addressed the situation; perhaps it is more appropriate to say he "undressed" the situation.

The religious people of Assisi assumed Francis had become mentally deranged from the beatings he took from the Muslim warriors. But in reality, it was a spiritual reformation that had taken place in Francis. This was a reformation that would change Francis, the church, and the world—for the better—forever.

Under compulsion from God and being undergirded by the Scriptures, Francis came before the church diocese in his community to express his faith. The priest and the leaders were arrayed in their richly adorned religious garments, which made Pietro happy to see, and it also made him filthy rich. The temple was a cold impersonal edifice, filled with ornate relics, statues, and stained glass. Worst of all, the people were proud of this form of religiosity. The hall echoed with the impersonal groans of Gregorian chanting. To call it music would be wanton disregard to grace and worship.

Francis humbly stood before his community, and from his heart, wanted them to know his love for them—but most importantly, he wanted them to know the personal love God had for them. He wanted them to know that God had made Himself known and could be known and enjoyed. He wanted everyone, rich and poor alike, to know that through Jesus and the Holy Spirit, they could find freedom and purpose for their lives.

Like Daniel before a den of lions, Francis stood before these religious people and struggled to explain these scriptural truths that meant so much to him. In his attempt to communicate, he began to undress himself. He stepped out of his expensive garment and slowly walked down the center aisle naked and out into a world that was waiting for him. One would think that it would be a cold and cruel world waiting to pounce on him, but God covered him in every way.

Francis walked to a dilapidated and abandoned church edifice in the country and began to practice what he had been preaching. He continued to worship God personally, enjoying God more and more in nature and in the Scripture study he devoted himself to. As he lived this way, simple songs began to flood his soul, and he sang them back to God. He was fulfilled and happy in God, and even though he was in abject poverty and obscurity, he was content.

It wasn't long before wandering souls made their way to Francis. The poor, lame, and mentally challenged were soon alongside him filling their lives with fellowship, worship, and ministry service. There were even old friends who traveled to see Francis to help him "come to his senses" and rethink his decision. But, to no avail, Francis knew that he had found his calling. Every week more misfits made their way to Francis, and, before long, there was a congregation of worshipers singing Scripture-filled songs in worship to God, and Francis was their troubadour. He would be known as "God's Troubadour." Out of this community came a sincere ministry in Jesus' name to the poor and needy. His followers took vows of celibacy, poverty, and purity. They were known for the joy of the Lord that filled them individually and as a community.

Francis was never interested in being commended by the "Church," but in time, he and his ministry were. They would be known as "Friars," would wear simple tunics, live lives of personal devotion to God, and would minister to the poor. Four hundred years later, his followers would reach Port Royal, Jamaica, and the story goes on, just like the beats in a song.

Peter was a Franciscan and was heading to America to help establish a ministry when his boat began to leak and had to stay for a while in Port Royal. Everyday a young black woman would come to him with a basket of fresh fruits and vegetables; her name was Lily. It wasn't long before Peter would renounce his celibacy and marry her. Though he never renounced his faith, he embraced the Christian teachings the Friars imparted to him and a relationship with God that meant so much to him.

Lily died giving birth to Esther, and Peter had the grace to continue the mission he began in Port Royal. As a good farmer, Peter kept his hands to the plow and didn't look back: God used him to begin a little Christian community of faithful followers of Jesus. Even though Tim had been *shanghaied* and was captive to the *Adventurer* and its rotten crew of smelly pirates, he, too, had been saved by grace and was now Peter's son-in-law and son in the faith. Tim and Esther had enjoyed a beautiful white waterfall wedding at Kings Falls, and a year later, they buried their miscarried son Ben. They had a tough start, as their new home was turned into a hospital for the sick and the dying after the Port Royal earthquake. They battled disease, grief, and mended lots of wounds as they lived "the normal Christian life."

Tim and his blacksmith friend Clay realized that the "wealth of the wicked" was in the water, for when the city sank into the sea, the gold and the silver was out in the bay, and they had determined to salvage this wealth. They undertook a reclamation project that raised more than enough *loot* to purchase the plantation Shalom and several buildings in Spanish Town. The little Christian community had been learning vital spiritual lessons from God's holy Word, and they were looking to the future. They were not only confident about God's presence in their midst, but were happy to serve their community and the "who-so-evers" God would bring their way.

Shalom, the plantation house, was large and had a wraparound porch with a detached kitchen. The kitchens in these parts were always detached to keep the heat away from the rest of the house. These people cherished the cool times and enjoyed the ocean breezes while they took siestas under the roof of the deck. During midday, this community would rest and avoid being out in the heat. They all had a mind to work and had quickly learned how to farm and ranch and raised up new homes for their people. The most unusual thing about this community was their love for God, and they showed it in their singing of worship songs. Tonight they are all gathered around the fire pit roasting chicken and singing "All Creatures of Our God and King":

> *All creatures of our God and King,*
> *Lift up your voice and with us sing,*
> *Alleluia, Alleluia!*
> *Thou burning sun with golden beam,*
> *Thou silver moon with softer gleam:*
> *O praise Him, O praise Him!*
> *Alleluia, Alleluia! Alleluia!*
> *Lift up your voices once again,*
> *And praise Him*
> *O Praise Him Alleluia!*
>
> *Thou rushing wind that art so strong,*
> *Ye clouds that sail in heav'n along,*
> *O praise Him! Alleluia!*
> *Thou rising morn in praise rejoice,*
> *Ye lights of evening, find a voice:*
> *O praise Him! Alleluia, Alleluia! Alleluia!*
>
> *Thou flowing water, pure and clear,*
> *Make music for thy Lord to hear,*
> *Alleluia, Alleluia!*
> *Thou fire so masterful and bright,*
> *That givest man both warmth and light,*
> *O praise Him! O praise Him! Alleluia, Alleluia! Alleluia!*
>
> *Let all things their Creator bless,*
> *And worship Him in humbleness—*
> *O praise Him! Alleluia!*
> *Praise, Praise the Father, Praise the Son,*
> *And praise the Spirit, Three in One:*
> *O praise Him, O praise Him! Alleluia, Alleluia! Alleluia!*

Papa Peter talked about how God has revealed Himself to His children through creation, His Son, His Spirit, and by His holy Word. The group affirmed this truth and spontaneously expressed their gratitude with outbursts of thanksgiving and praise. He also reminded them that Jesus used nature to teach wonderful spiritual lessons and that Francis did the same. He let them know that it was Francis who wrote the song they had just sung and encouraged them to think uplifting thoughts. He said, "We are privileged to work with God as we work this land. Let's let Him speak to us, and let's use our work as a *shove-off* to worship." The group affirmed the message and retired for the evening, leaving the coals to flicker.

As moths are attracted to flame, many new souls were being drawn to the plantation they called Shalom. The community of believers was overjoyed to see their fellowship enlarge, and Papa was reminded that, just as Francis left that cold religious edifice in Assisi, Italy, it wasn't long before people began showing up on his doorstep. It seemed like every day, God was adding to their number. At their Wednesday worship and Bible study time, the group was singing:

> *Sowing in the morning, sowing seeds of kindness,*
> *Sowing in the noontide and the dewy eve,*
> *Waiting for the harvest and the time of reaping—*
> *We shall come rejoicing, bringing in the sheaves.*
>
> *Bringing in the sheaves, bringing in the sheaves,*
> *We shall come rejoicing, bringing in the sheaves.*

> *Bringing in the sheaves, bringing in the sheaves,*
> *We shall come rejoicing, bringing in the sheaves.*
>
> *Sowing in the sunshine, sowing in the shadows,*
> *Fearing nether clouds nor winter's chilling breeze;*
> *By and by the harvest and the labor ended—*
> *We shall come rejoicing, bringing in the sheaves.*
>
> *Going forth with weeping, sowing for the Master,*
> *Tho the loss sustained our spirit often grieves;*
> *When our weeping's over, He will bid us welcome—*
> *We shall come rejoicing, bringing in the sheaves.*
>
> *Bringing in the sheaves, bringing in the sheaves,*
> *We shall come rejoicing, bringing in the sheaves.*
> *Bringing in the sheaves, bringing in the sheaves.*
> *We shall come rejoicing, bringing in the sheaves.*

Tim applauded their singing and commented: "It is wonderful to see how God has led us and provided for our needs. We know it is not about us. It is about God's glory and the sheaves. He wants to reach the lost. Working out in the sugar cane fields, we have been bundling up the stocks into sheaves, and it looks like God is doing the same in our fellowship." The congregation collectively looked around to one another, nodded their heads, smiled, and welcomed in the strangers. They were happy that new people had found their way to the community.

The next day Tim, Esther, Wyndolyn, Chase, Christina, Earl, Nick, and Clay met with Papa Peter under the magnolia tree far from earshot, so they could have a conversation about their changing community. Wyndolyn was most animated as she spoke: "You all know how I love to cook, but I can't afford to feed all these hungry faces. I don't have the energy, the pots, and pans, or enough food to feed this crowd. But what really grates me is that these new people just presume that they will be fed. What word has gone out that lets them think that food is free here? When I had Breezy's Café, I made some darn good *loot* cooking for my customers."

Earl was quick to agree and said: "Don't get me wrong. It is great to see our group grow, but they just sit back and watch me and my horses work. There is plenty of work to do, and it doesn't take much training to plant, weed, and pull in the harvest. All it takes is the will to work and some elbow grease." The group laughed and was amazed because Earl wasn't one to ever speak out.

Papa listened to everyone and, to his surprise, he found that each one had a story of being taken advantage of by the newcomers. After he had heard the concerns, he said: "I have been praying about what we are to study from the Bible, and now I know it clear. We need wisdom. God has given us a book specific to this need: It is called the book of Proverbs. It is a collection of pithy wisdom thoughts that will help us deal with these situations. Do you all agree? We need wisdom!"

Chase volunteered his thoughts: "When I was on a ship— even though it was a pirate ship—we still had a democracy, and everyone knew they that had work to do, and they did it. If they didn't, they got smartened up. *Picaroons were a scurvy* to the ship, even a pirate ship. You know what I mean? Now we love everyone that has come to Shalom, but should we let him or her stay the way they are? I don't want to revert to my old pirate ways, but shouldn't we love them enough to help them and help our families? We need to get in *shipshape, aye!*"

The group laughed and agreed; then Christina began to testify. "You all know how I was swept up off the streets in London, shipped to Port Royal, and forced to work in the sex trade. If it weren't for God's grace, Esther and Wyndolyn loving me, accepting me, and helping me to learn other things to do, the pirates would still be *pillaging* me! At least they paid for my services. I tell you, we have to *avast* this situation. There are *freebooters* here, and we have to help them learn new trades and new attitudes."

The group was amazed with the maturity and the grace Christina possessed. Papa chimed in by saying: "Christina, Chase, you get it; you have understanding. You have wisdom. The first step to gaining wisdom is the humility to acknowledge that we need it. Wisdom is not just having the information, knowing the story, but it is understanding God's Word and then applying it to our life situation. Solomon was considered the wisest person who has ever lived. God appeared to him in a dream and asked, 'What do you want? And I will give it to you!' Do you know what Solomon asked for?" The group wanted to know more; their eyes begged for the rest of the story.

Papa said: "Solomon asked God for an understanding heart, so he could govern well and know the difference between right and wrong. God was so impressed with Solomon for his un-pirate like request, that He honored his request and gave him extraordinary wisdom. This wisdom is in a collection called the Proverbs. We will treasure it, and it will lead us as we humbly ask God to help us grow this community He is building here."

Esther had encouragement all over her face. She smiled and said, "I think this is the same situation St. Francis was in after he made his wonderful discoveries." Papa agreed saying, "And Jesus, too, had an unusual band of followers that were attracted to Him. We all are a bunch of misfits that Jesus has caused to fit into His body." Nick jumped into the conversation: "I, too, had been on a slew of pirate ships. I am a *landlubber* now, and it is a new day trying to learn how to work the land. When a person is out at sea, you learned how to meet your own needs with your *boucon,* your sharp tongue, and *hornswoggling* was the way to get what you wanted. Now that we are in Christ, we can't let 'the little pirate,' or a bunch of little pirates ruin us. We have to learn new ways and help others walk in these ways."

Tim shouted, "Amen, brother." And Papa Peter said: "I think you will discover that the book of Proverbs is very much in touch with the ways of the little pirate.

I know some of the words it explains you are familiar with, like *slackers, sloths, saggars,* and *sluggards.*" Nick and Chase laughed, and Frieda squawked. Nick asked, "Are those words in the Proverbs?" Papa said: "Yes, and it explains them well. The Proverbs have a purpose: They will teach us wisdom and discipline. They will help us to understand the insights of the truly wise. They will show us how to be successful, and how to do what is right and just. They will show us that the fear of the Lord is the foundation of true knowledge and that pirates have always despised wisdom and discipline." Tim said, "Ain't that the truth!"

Papa lamented, "We need God's help in building these people up and in building community. We need to learn how to build relationships, how to get along with each other, how to help 'misfits' fit. How to identify and deal with pirates, how to make a living legitimately, and how to make the most out of what we have. It will teach us how to deal with the *loot* and to take responsibility for our lives. It will guide us as we try to raise our children in the 'fear of the Lord.' I am confident knowing that, if we seek after wisdom, we will have it, as God will not withhold any good thing from those who walk uprightly. I am confident, if we choose responsibility in time, we will become respected and have a good influence in our community."

The group seemed to know that this discussion had come to an end; they all felt as if they had been heard and that God was going to meet their real needs with real wisdom. Some of the group began to disperse from the shade of the magnolia tree, but a few hung back to ask a few questions about some of the new people who had made their way to Shalom. Papa had seen a man that he swore he had seen before in Port Royal. He looked different, but the *swagger* was still in his step. He asked about him; those who remained had lots of questions about those new to their group. The consent was unanimous: They agreed that they needed to get to know these new people and try to show them God's love and acceptance.

BASK: Wisdom

Papa and the leaders at Shalom began to collect what they called **"Gold Nuggets of Wisdom."** Here is the first bagful.

- Walk with the wise and grow wise (Proverbs 13:20).
- A person of good sense is respected.
- The rut of routine can be the groove of grace.
- The battle is always to believe the truth.
- Believers are always positive because faith in God is a positive thing.
- Consider it joy when you encounter trials because they are the ordained exercise you need to become strong (James 1:1–3; Romans 5:3–6).
- It is not about being perfect; it is about joining God in the process.
- Everything in moderation; be temperate.
- "As now, so then." If you want to do something great, work to that end today. There is no time like the present. The "present' is a gift; unwrap it now!
- Don't let Satan lick the sugar off your candy by getting you to dwell on past failures. Tell Jesus to remind him about his future, and as for you, you think about Glory!
- The only debt you should owe is the debt of love (Romans 13:8).
- Be thankful for what you do have. Thanksgiving is "the key to everything."

Fool's Gold: It looks shiny, but it is worthless. Beware of fool's gold just as you should beware of pirates. It is also called *pyrite*—funny how it is a lot like a pirate. *Aaaargh!*

- Entitlement: Do not live expecting anything from the government, the world, family, or friends.
- Props: Just because a pirate has gold chains, the red silk suit, the brass-toed boots, a shiny *boucon*, and a blunderbuss gun doesn't mean he has anything of real value.
- Fool's gold is just "pyrite!" How are pirates and pyrite alike?
- Chase with pirates. (Then your ship will sink.)
- Be like a fish and chase the glittering lures.
- Live for yourself. (Pirates will always *maroon you, keelhaul you,* make you *walk the plank,* or make you *kiss the gunner's daughter.*)
- Fake like you care. A pirate will fake like he cares about you, but beware: He will *scupper* you.
- Always be intrigued by the gold that glitters. (But, remember this: All that glitters is not gold. Fish are attracted to and then snared by shiny lures that have a hook in them. Do not let shiny objects keep you from what has real value.)

2.

Beware of Pirates

Without saying a word, this little community was growing up. People from all over the area seemed to understand that there was an invitation to come to Shalom and find hope, peace, love, and acceptance.

The people collected the torn sails from ships and were using them to build tents on the property. They also brought with them the language of sailors and pirates, and more misfits were added to the misfits that already made up this assembly.

On the grounds, you could see evidence of a rough life, as it wasn't unusual to see a peg leg, an eye patch from a lost eye, or a hook where a hand used to be. There were lots of scars, and, surely, there were lots of sad stories to be told.

Just because there was infiltration didn't mean there wasn't excitement for growth and joy in the community—there was. But, Papa and the leaders of Shalom were concerned, as they knew that influence is not neutral, and they wanted to make sure the "fear of the Lord" was the pre-eminent influence in the community. Papa wasn't about to leave peer pressure to chance. He called some extra meetings, so this society could be integrated with Christian values.

At these meetings there was singing of Christian songs, prayer, and fellowship with food. There was a welcoming and hospitable attitude. However, Papa got right to the point. He said, "I welcome all of you to Shalom. We have been praying for God to add to our numbers. We exist for the glory of the Lord and to let everyone know that God loves you and that Jesus died for you to bring you into His family of faith. We exist to wear the CROWN and to help others wear the CROWN.

"There are lots of new things waiting for all of us as our community grows. So let me establish who we are and what we are all about. You come by your own free will, and you will stay by our own free will. We will not try to force you to stay or force you to believe. You have probably had enough 'force' in your lives already!" Chase and Nick shouted, "Amen, preach it!"

Papa continued, "As for who we are, we wear the CROWN, and this is what we will teach and live. Some of you sailed for a crown, but when we talk about the

CROWN, we are referencing Jesus who is the one true King. We seek to wear His crown of thorns and to remember His suffering, service, and sacrifice for us. We also hope everyone will understand their true identity in His gold, kingly, and jeweled crown and appreciate what He left to come to us—but also what He is making of us, as we are a kingdom of priests, kings, and true royalty for Him.

"CROWN stands for Christ who is our life. Righteousness is the miracle that happened when we first believed in Jesus, as he took rotten sinners and turned us into saints. Order is established in our lives, as we learn to let Jesus have His rule and reign in us. The King is in residence here!" The congregation let out a cheer, and then Papa continued.

"We live to worship God. This is our purpose and our commitment. We intend to worship our way through every problem, every possibility, and with every praise. We intend to give God thanks in all things, because we believe this is the key to everything. And we will walk in nobility, acknowledging that God is here and seeking to honor Him with the way we live and the way we relate to each other.

"This is what it means to wear the CROWN. Those of you who are new to us, I encourage you to make this your topic of conversation—and feel free to talk with anyone who has been here awhile. This is who we are, and this is most important to us. You might be asking why this is so crucial to us? It is very simple. Behavior and attitude flow from identity—and if your identity isn't right—your behavior will 'feed the fish,' or should I say 'feed the flesh.' In time you will understand what I am saying. But, we all know that the 'little pirate' in us only seeks to ruin us, and we all know what the little pirate is. *Aye!*"

Chase shouted, "The little pirate is our flesh, ARRGH!"

Frieda, his pet parrot, squawked with glee. The community erupted with laughter.

Papa was laughing with joy, and he said, "Those of you who are new need to get ahold of what our values are and work with us. If you have questions, you can discuss with us as we are not *addled* here. You won't have to fear *walking the plank* or being *marooned* if you don't understand or disagree with us. But, what we do ask for is respect and for you to keep short accounts. Do not let bad feelings fester. Those of you who were once on pirate ships know that you were always threatened with rejection. We believe that is what enflames the flesh. Aka, the little pirate in us. Our aim is to build a community around love and acceptance that is rooted in God's forgiveness, demonstrated by Jesus Christ and His sacrificial death on the cross.

"With that said, we do have expectations. Though they are few, we ask you to buy in to them. If you can't, you are free to leave, but we ask you to do so peacefully. Our expectations are few and simple. We expect everyone to participate in our weekly Bible study and worship service. We expect everyone to participate in our community life. No person is an island unto himself or herself. We are on an island, but no one is to act like an island, as we need each other. You are expected to grow as a person. And, you are expected to care for this community. You are also expected to give to this community. When I say give, I am not just talking about the *pieces of eight* in your pocket. We believe the good Lord has given each one spiritual gifts, and we are all called to serve. We are all expected to work.

"The other day, I mentioned to some of our group the words, *slacker*, *sloth*, *saggar*, and *sluggard*. Let me explain. Some of you have been seriously injured, and there is little you can do, but find what you can do and help. If you can peel potatoes, peel them for the glory of God and the good of our community. We don't want anyone here to be a *slacker*. The Proverbs state that he who has a 'slack' hand becomes poor. It also says the sloth is cast into a deep sleep, so don't be like a *sloth*. Elsewhere, the Bible tells of a person whose roof sags because they didn't build it up. So don't be a *saggar* and let your britches slide down your rump. And it warns against the *sluggard*. The Proverbs tell us that the fields of the lazy man are overgrown with weeds. We can't afford sloppy behavior, and being slack is not allowed. So, encourage everyone daily to work hard. Many a pirate became a pirate because he really didn't want to work. Beware of pirates! Around here we have a commitment to work, and we are grateful that we have work to do. We hope to put our harvested goods out on the *trade winds* and make a good living here. I promise we will work at our work, and we will enjoy playing at our play. This is the way to the abundant life Jesus promised."

The group was encouraged by what Papa had to say. Papa felt that enough had been said and thanked them for their attention, and then he thanked the women and a few of the men who helped bake the mango pies and brewed the sweet tea for their efforts. After a word of prayer laced with thanksgiving, the group gathered around the tables by the kitchen and on the porch of Shalom.

The next day, Papa went searching for the man who struck his imagination. He recognized the *swagger*, but didn't know if this *bucko* was a *swashbuckler* or not. Nevertheless Papa was usually proactive, so that he wouldn't have to be reactive to problems. He was known to say, "An ounce of prevention is worth a pound of cure." Today he had seen the man with the wide-brimmed straw hat, the reed of grass in his mouth, the breeches that gathered under his knees, and with the stockings and buckled shoes. The white linen shirt was common to these parts, but the strong Scottish accent wasn't. This man wasn't motley; he wasn't mismatched in any way, but Papa was sure that he was someone he had seen before—and he believed that he needed to know if he were up to no good.

This man wasn't hard to find; he was out in the open helping Earl work with his horses and learning to farm sugar cane. As a matter of fact, he seemed to know what he was doing, and Earl seemed to be enjoying his help and his company. Papa walked out into the cane field, and Earl introduced Papa to his new friend, Reo, saying, "We have a newbie here who wants to be a *landlubber.* Papa, I want you to meet Reo. He seems to know how to farm and likes to work real good." Reo stepped up to shake Papa's hand, and with a deep Scottish accent said, "Happy to meet you, man. I liked what you said at the meetin' last eve." Papa, not wanting to mess around, said, "I think I recognize you; let's head over to the magnolia tree, as I want to hear your story."

Reo seemed to wince, and then he took his hat off, wiped his brow, and said, "Let's chat." They quickly but quietly made their way to the tree, and from the porch, Esther began to walk toward them with a jar of sweet tea and a couple of glasses. After cordial greetings, Papa asked, "Reo, where did I first see you?" Reo answered, "I don't know. I have only spent a little time on this island." Papa said, "I think I recognize you, and I think I might have seen you in Port Royal. I am not as concerned about your past as I am concerned about your aims. Maybe that is where we should start?" Reo said, "That is a good thing because there is a bunch of bad information about me floating around the Caribbean. But I tell you the truth: All I really want to do is farm and live a quiet, peaceful life."

Papa affirmed Reo and added, "I believe with all my heart that everyone has a past, and that is not who you really are. In fact, the devil always brings it up, and I don't want to be like him. I believe God has a good future for you, and this is what I want to be about. I want to help you attain the glorious future God has for you." Feeling relieved and seeing the love on Papa's face, Reo took the grass out of his mouth and said, "I was in Port Royal on that fateful day. I say 'fateful,' but truthfully the earthquake saved my life." Papa said, "How can that be? Thousands died." Reo answered, "I know, but it saved me. I was in the Port Royal Prison. I was to be hanged, as a kangaroo court quickly tried me and sentenced me to die." Papa, not wanting to dwell on this man's past, said, "I know these things can happen." Reo nodded his head and said, "I was accused of being a pirate, but I tell you the truth: My crew and I did steal, but we really didn't function as pirates." Papa didn't know how to respond, but thinking that wisdom remains quiet, he remained silent for a while, and then he said, "I know life can be unfair." Reo laughed, and with joy exclaimed, "But God is good. That tidal wave washed me out of the dungeon of despair, and in no time, I was in the middle of the harbor swimming. I swam out to a whaling ship and found a good crew. I was saved and enjoyed whaling. God always has the last laugh." Papa laughed and said, "This sounds outlandish, but I just want your word that you won't be pirate-like against us." Reo said, "I give you my word: I will not be pirate-like. I have no desire to take anything from anyone." Papa said, "That sounds like another story." Reo asked, "All I want is to farm and be part of a caring community. Will you respect my desire?" Papa said, "I will, but you have to let me in to your life. I need to hear your story, and I want to help you grow in your faith." Their eyes sparkled their agreement. Shaking hands and giving gentlemen's hugs, they agreed to regularly meet under the magnolia tree for tea and for talks.

The Wednesday evening Bible study and worship time came quickly because of all the activity in Shalom. Most everyone could gather in the plantation house, but some had to spill over into the entryway, and others sat in the windowsills or just outside the windows to participate as much as possible. Everyone could see the need for a large barn to facilitate the church meetings.

As usual there was lots of singing and joking around, as everyone was happy to be together. The excitement was high because they were looking forward to getting to know the new people. Esther and Clay were leading the music, as both had beautiful voices and the leadership to direct the group. Esther had the mandolin out and was strumming to set the beat. They introduced the group to a new song, so Esther and Clay sang it first for the group to learn. Then after discussing the words, they sang it as a large choir:

> *All people that on the earth do dwell,*
> *Sing to the Lord with cheerful voice;*
> *Him serve with mirth,*
> *His praise forth tell,*
> *Come ye before Him and rejoice.*

Know that the Lord is God indeed:
Without our aid He did us make;
We are His folk, He doth us feed,
And for His sheep He doth us take.

O enter then His gates with praise,
Approach with joy His courts unto;
Praise, laud, and bless His name always,
For it is seemly so to do.

For why? The Lord our God is good,
His mercy is forever sure;
His truth at all times firmly stood,
And shall from age to age endure.
Amen!

Papa had some handwritten sheets in front of him that contained some of the Wisdom Literature he was planning to talk about. Without saying a word of greeting, he began to pray. His prayer was filled with unction, and the group was raptured by their time before the throne of grace. Then Papa said, "We have all lived around pirates; we have all been fearful of pirates, and we have learned to beware of pirates. And even personally, we have to chastise the little pirate in us. God knows how to deal with pirates. Solomon, in the book of Proverbs, speaks to this concern and provides the remedy.

"We all know that 'bad company corrupts good morals,' but do you know good from bad, and right from wrong? Do you know how to discern a *privateer* from a *pirate*? I tell you the Word of God is helpful here. God has given us His Word. It is given by inspiration, and it is profitable for teaching the truth, for reproof, for correction, and for instruction in righteousness. It is given to build us up for every good work. Often it will show us our pirate-like ways, and then it will crucify that little pirate, so we can live free. It is interesting that men go into piracy to try to live free, but I tell you, real freedom is found by being a slave to Jesus. It takes wisdom to find true freedom."

The congregation cheered this little rant, and then they listened attentively.

Papa then introduced the topic of wisdom by saying, "Pirates play on our fears … pirates have lots to fear. They fear the Kraken, alligators, and crocodiles. They fear *walking the plank* or being *marooned*. They dread the *doldrums;* they get eerie at the thought of going near Bermuda, and they are afraid to get close to a woman. Oh, they want to raise the *Jolly Roger* and have their jollies, but to be known and to care, *shivers their timbers* with fear. They really are a fearful lot. In the book of Proverbs, chapter one, King Solomon describes pirates. I have asked Tim to read this passage."

Tim stood up, went to the center of the room, cleared his throat, and cited:

10
My son, if sinners entice you,
Do not consent.

11
If they say, "Come with us,
Let us lie in wait to *shed* blood;
Let us lurk secretly for the innocent without cause;
12
Let us swallow them alive like Sheol,
And whole, like those who go down to the Pit;
13
We shall find all *kinds* of precious possessions,
We shall fill our houses with spoil;
14
Cast in your lot among us,
Let us all have one purse"—
15
My son, do not walk in the way with them,
Keep your foot from their path;
16
For their feet run to evil,
And they make haste to shed blood.
17
Surely, in vain the net is spread
In the sight of any bird;
18
But they lie in wait for their *own* blood,
They lurk secretly for their *own* lives.
19
So *are* the ways of everyone who is greedy for gain;
It takes away the life of its owners.
(Proverbs 1:10–19)

Papa thanked Tim for reading the Bible text, and then he commented, "Pirates are sinners in that they always try to meet their needs in their own way. They are quick to strike with their *boucon* or head for the ship, raise their sails, and sail. They relish raising the *Jolly Roger* and sacking an unsuspecting crew. We all know that they will do the same to you. And some of you have lived like this, too. In a very real way, we all have the little pirate in us. Just know that God understands pirates and their ways, and He doesn't look the other way.

"Pirates are in the recruiting business, and they try to get others to violate their consciences and join them in their illicit activities. Influence is never neutral, so 'beware of pirates.' They are greedy for gain; this is why it is so important for us to be a community of givers. We want the current of grace to flow through us, and, in humility, we want to make personal sacrifices for the good of the community and the onlooking world. This is so anti-pirate. Solomon gives us six specific things to look for when you think you see a pirate in yourself or others. This is from Proverbs, chapter six. I will quote:

16
These six *things* the Lord hates,
Yes, seven *are* an abomination to Him:
17
A proud look,
A lying tongue,
Hands that shed innocent blood,

18
A heart that devises wicked plans,
Feet that are swift in running to evil,
19
A false witness *who* speaks lies,
And one who sows discord among brethren.
(Proverbs 6:16–19)

"As we go to God in prayer, I will repeat this passage again, and I ask you to let the Holy Spirit have His way with you. If He convicts you of any of these attitudes, I want you to say, 'Thank you, Lord, that I am not a pirate. Please align my life with Jesus who is my true life and my true identity. Amen!'"

Gold Nuggets of Wisdom:

- Those who hate wisdom love death (Proverbs 8:36)!
- The "fear of the LORD" is the most valuable thing you own.
- The "fear of man" is a snare. Beware of pirate types that pressure you. Peer pressure can be overcome by reckoning that you are "accepted in the Beloved" (Ephesians 1:6)!
- When they say it is not about the *loot,* it is usually about the *loot!*
- True riches are found in faith, hope, and love. It is good to have *loot*—because *loot* can buy you things—but, in reality, it is more valuable to possess the things *loot* cannot buy. Think about it!
- Take care of what you own, but make sure that it doesn't "own" you.
- Pick your friends well, as "bad company corrupts good morals" (1 Corinthians 15:33).
- You can't tell a book by its cover.

Fool's Gold:

- A proud look
- A lying tongue
- A wicked plan
- An unrealistic expectation
- A promise without a plan
- An unfaithful friend
- Look and act like a *swashbuckler*; have that famous *swagger* strut of pirates.
- *Splicing the main brace* will make you feel rich. (But, drinking rum will get you to waste away what you worked so hard to acquire.)
- Compensatory spending is wasting *Pieces of Eight* on *grog* that will make you feel rich for a moment. (But, in time you won't have any silver or gold in your pouch. Don't be stupid and spend good money on junk that will help you "compensate" for feelings of inadequacy, inferiority, insecurity, or insignificance. Know this: You are truly complete in Christ (Colossians 2:6–10).

3.

The "Real" Pearl Story

Reo had been working very hard to help Earl plant and harvest sugar cane. He had been helping everyone and tried diligently to befriend everyone and was overly nice to all. This behavior had Papa concerned. He was suspicious and earnestly desired to meet with Reo to see what was really going on. Papa had met many a pirate in his day. He didn't know if Reo was one or not, but he was noticing a serious pirate-like "flesh tendency." For some reason, Papa was concerned about Reo. Reo was clearly liked by most everyone at Shalom, but Papa had his eye on him.

In the kitchen, Reo would stay after dinner to help clean the pots and the pans. Out in the field, Reo was eager to help everyone plant and pick. Reo even went to visit Clay and Tim in the blacksmith shop where, in one of the burned-out buildings downtown, they were setting up the forge. Reo helped them set up their shop and enjoyed learning about blacksmithing. It seemed as if he cared to get to know everyone and displayed an amiable attitude. Papa was paying attention and thought he was trying to earn favor, prove his worth, or worse—that he was forming alliances. Like a fisherman with a spear, Papa took dead aim and confronted Reo in his tent. He invited him to join him again under the mahogany tree for some tea and conversation.

Papa commended Reo for all the hard work he had noticed, and Reo thought for sure that this was earning him some favor. But, to Reo's surprise, Papa questioned his motives about why he was working so hard and wondered what he was trying to prove. All of a sudden, their relationship changed as Reo became defensive.

Reo asked Papa, "Why is my work a cause of concern for you? Hard work has always been my way to establish myself in whatever community I am in." Papa nodded his head in agreement and said, "Our community is a lot different than most communities. Sure we value hard work, but we don't have to try to earn anything." Reo was taken aback and his thoughts were *scuppered*. He became quiet and didn't know how to respond. Reo shrugged his shoulders in bewilderment and asked, "Why is it that you are concerned about me when you see how hard I work? Work has always worked for me."

Papa smiled a big accepting smile and said, "That is exactly the point. I think that you think that your hard work is going to put you into our good graces." Reo nodded his head in agreement and said, "Isn't that how it works here?" Papa smiled again and said, "We appreciate hard work, and entitlement is not what we are about; we are about grace."

Reo said, "Are you saying that you don't want me to do anything?" Papa said, "That is not what I am saying. What I want to know is, are you doing all this hard work to gain our acceptance?" Reo said, "Yes, this is what I know, and what I would expect from someone new to my crew."

Papa grinned and said, "This is what I thought. I don't blame you as I am sure this is what you have learned. Please let me tell you a parable Jesus taught, and then you can tell me what you think He was saying." Reo smiled and uttered, "ARRRR." They both laughed, and Papa told about the parable of the hidden treasure and the pearl of great price. He recalled this gem from his memory:

The Parable of the Hidden Treasure

"Again, the kingdom of heaven is like treasure
hidden in a field, which a man found and
hid; and for joy over it he goes and sells
all that he has and buys that field."

The Parable of the Pearl of Great Price

"Again, the kingdom of heaven is like a
merchant seeking beautiful pearls, who, when
he had found one pearl of great price, went
and sold all that he had and bought it."
(Matthew 13:45–46)

Papa could tell that Reo was intrigued by the parable, so he asked, "What do you think it says, and what do you think it means?" Reo responded straightforwardly, "Like a pirate seeing the treasure they want; they then chase and raise the *Jolly Roger* and go and get it. They give all that they have to take it over. That must have been a special pearl to give it all for one pearl." Papa asked, "What do you think the pearl is in the story?" Reo shrugged and then uttered, "I think the pearl is faith in Jesus. If we work real hard, we can get Him: He *is* the pearl of great price."

Papa smiled and said, "Reo, that is what I thought you were going to say. That is what religion is all about, and we are not about religion." Reo was so flustered and dumbfounded, he could hardly speak. He stammered and said, "I thought I had it right. I didn't grow up in church or with a Christian faith. I just thought it was all about Jesus." Papa encouraged him by saying, "It is all about Jesus, but religion is what people do to earn love, acceptance, and forgiveness. The grace that Jesus came to teach us is what He has done for us. You see, you are the 'pearl of great price.' Jesus came to give His life for you. There is nothing you can do to deserve His love, acceptance, or forgiveness. It is called grace, if you believe you have nothing to prove and nothing to earn."

Reo was wide-eyed and amazed. He asked, "You mean I don't have to do anything to earn a place in this community or heaven?" Papa was profound, "That is the truth you must *avast!*" Reo opined, "Don't people just take advantage of you, Shalom, and God?" Papa laughed and then spoke, "Sure, some do, but those who truly believe give because they want to—not because they have to. What makes Shalom, 'Shalom,' is that people here are free to give, free to love, free to worship. We believe there is nothing to earn, and that we don't deserve anything. We simply live 'thank-you' lives to God."

Reo said, "That is totally different from what I grew up with." Papa said, "I thought so, but before I hear more of your story, let me ask you if you believe this." Reo said, "I want to believe it. I know religion really doesn't work." Papa agreed and then asked Reo to confirm this faith with a prayer. Reo was happy to join hands with Papa and pray to Jesus, thanking Jesus for the salvation provided by His grace alone!

Papa asked, "Please tell me about your life to this point, and what has shaped your beliefs?" Reo nodded and then dove in to his life story, "I was born in Barbados. My parents were Scottish slaves. My father got caught up in the English Civil War and ended up on the losing side. Cromwell didn't care, took my parents as slaves. It was brutal; they died young. I was orphaned as a boy. I was sold to a slave master who took delight in beating me, especially if I didn't work hard." Papa interrupted, "See how you learned to earn things with hard work—you made work 'work' for you." Reo opened his eyes very large and said, "I had never seen it like that before, but it is true: I learned to make hard work 'work' for me." Papa said, "Please continue. Your story is very interesting."

Reo went on, "I had to get away from this evil taskmaster, so in my early teens, I was a strong swimmer. I jumped into the Carlisle Bay and swam to freedom, or so I hoped. I was hopeful to find a good ship and crew, but I ended up going from bad to worse. I made my way onto the ship. Thoughtful crewmembers stowed me away. This ship was led by the notorious Captain Hawkins, who was a cruel pirate. He tortured his slaves, beat, and raped women. Even after we would overtake other ships, he left the crew *marooned*. Yet, his crew remained loyal to him. I guess it was because he had a history of making us rich. I hated him even though he captured great treasures and made his crew prosperous. I, too, have seen some pearls of great price, or, should I say, the great prize that was paid for pearls." When he talked about the pearls his eyes sparkled, and then he blushed. Papa just knew there was more to this story. Papa interrupted, "I want you to know I appreciate your past, but what is most important for you to know is that because of God's rich grace for you, you will have a glorious future! Just know that I exist to help people discover true freedom by appropriating the power of a true identity." As soon as Papa said "true identity," Reo covered his face as if he were a real loser. It became quiet, and then Papa asked, "Did I offend you?" Reo mumbled, "I need to tell you who I really am." Papa said, "I think I know who you really are. I believe in you because I believe God brought you here, and He has begun a good work in you. Don't let the enemy get you to believe any of his lies. Like what you have lived or done determines who you are. I believe you are a child of the one true King. Will you let me help you discover true treasure, the treasure of your true identity?" Reo felt the love and said, "Yes!" They hugged, and Papa reminded Reo about the Wednesday evening Bible study and worship time. They agreed to meet later in the week under the magnolia tree.

Wednesday evening arrived, and everyone in Shalom was eager to meet for fellowship, worship, prayer, and Bible study. Papa had Tim read the Bible text because he was training him to be a Bible teacher. Tim read the following:

Guidance for the Young

1
My son, do not forget my law,
But let your heart keep my commands;
2
For length of days and long life
And peace they will add to you.

3
Let not mercy and truth forsake you;
Bind them around your neck,
Write them on the tablet of your heart,
4
And so find favor and high esteem
In the sight of God and man.
5
Trust in the LORD with all your heart,
And lean not on your own understanding;
6
In all your ways acknowledge Him,
And He shall direct your paths.
7
Do not be wise in your own eyes;
Fear the LORD and depart from evil.
8
It will be health to your flesh,
And strength to your bones.
9
Honor the LORD with your possessions,
And with the firstfruits of all your increase;
10
So your barns will be filled with plenty,
And your vats will overflow with new wine.
11
My son, do not despise the chastening of the LORD,
Nor detest His correction;
12
For whom the LORD loves He corrects,
Just as a father the son *in whom* he delights.

13
Happy *is* the man *who* finds wisdom,
And the man *who* gains understanding;
14
For her proceeds *are* better than the profits of silver,
And her gain than fine gold.
15
She *is* more precious than rubies,
And all the things you may desire
cannot compare with her.
16
Length of days *is* in her right hand,
In her left hand riches and honor.
17
Her ways *are* ways of pleasantness,
And all her paths *are* peace.
18
She *is* a tree of life to those who take hold of her,
And happy *are all* who retain her.
19
The LORD by wisdom founded the earth;
By understanding He established the heavens;
20
By His knowledge the depths were broken up,
And clouds drop down the dew.
21
My son, let them not depart from your eyes—
Keep sound wisdom and discretion;
22
So they will be life to your soul
And grace to your neck.

23
Then you will walk safely in your way,
And your foot will not stumble.
24
When you lie down, you will not be afraid;
Yes, you will lie down and your sleep will be sweet.
25
Do not be afraid of sudden terror,
Nor of trouble from the wicked when it comes;
26
For the LORD will be your confidence,
And will keep your foot from being caught.
27
Do not withhold good from those to whom it is due,
When it is in the power of your hand to do *so*.
28
Do not say to your neighbor,
"Go, and come back,
And tomorrow I will give *it*,"
When *you have* it with you.
29
Do not devise evil against your neighbor,
For he dwells by you for safety's sake.
30
Do not strive with a man without cause,
If he has done you no harm.
31
Do not envy the oppressor,
And choose none of his ways;

32
For the perverse *person is* an abomination to the Lord,
But His secret counsel *is* with the upright.
33
The curse of the Lord *is* on the house of the wicked,
But He blesses the home of the just.
34
Surely He scorns the scornful,
But gives grace to the humble.
35
The wise shall inherit glory,
But shame shall be the legacy of fools.
(Proverbs 3: 1–35)

As usual, Papa took the time to go over the text verse by verse. Tonight he dwelled on verse five. He was especially animated to impress this little congregation about the importance of showing that we trust God and to not lean on our own understanding. He made it clear that pirates choose to meet their own needs in their own ways—and that was "leaning on their own understanding." He used the text once again to tell the group that this is what sin is in a very real way. But, the main focus of his teaching was about living out of the "tree of life," and not the "tree of the knowledge of good and evil." He used this teaching to take the group to the tree where Jesus died and explained how it became the tree of life. He defined the grace of God and let everyone know that Jesus' sacrificial death on the cross took care of all our sins—past, present, and future. He wanted everyone to know that they were under the grace of God and not under cruel laws anymore. Because of this, he explained how they were now "accepted in the Beloved" (Ephesians 1:6) and didn't have to work to gain God's acceptance. Papa mentioned that, because God loves us this way, we, too, love each other and try to release God's grace in our relationships to one another.

The group enjoyed a good season of prayer, and then Esther began to sing "Praise, My Soul, the King of Heaven":

> *Praise, my soul, the King of heaven,*
> *To His feet thy tribute bring;*
> *Ransomed, healed, restored, forgiven,*
> *Evermore His praises sing;*
> *Allelluia! Alleluia!!*
> *Praise the everlasting King!*
>
> *Praise Him for His grace and favor*
> *To our fathers in distress;*
> *Praise Him, still the same as ever,*
> *Slow to chide,*
> *And swift to bless.*
> *Allelluia! Allelluia!*
> *Glorious in His faithfulness.*
>
> *Frail as summer's flower we flourish,*
> *Blows the wind and it is gone;*
> *But, while mortals rise and perish,*
> *God endures unchanging on.*
> *Allelluia! Allelluia!*
> *Praise the High Eternal One.*

Angels in the height, adore Him;
Ye behold him face to face;
Saints triumphant, bow before Him,
Gathered in from every race;
Allelluia! Allelluia!
Praise with us the God of grace.
Amen.

After the service and during the fellowship time, Reo sought out Papa and asked him if he were speaking to him. Papa said, "It only feels that way. God's Word has a way of speaking to us all, all the time. It is living and active."

BASK: *Wisdom*

Gold Nuggets of Wisdom:

- All God's children have been blessed with spiritual gifts. The Holy Spirit will use mature believers to help you discover your spiritual gifts, how to unwrap them, and put them to use for God's glory.
- Pride will push people away from you; your humility will attract people to you.
- Your entrance into the lives of others might not be your gifts or your successes: It may be your failures and struggles.
- Wisdom is discovered in many counselors. Learn to look for the sage people in your world and then walk with them to grow wise.
- Wisdom flows from your true identity. Know that Jesus is your life and true identity. If you believe this, soon you will be living like Him (Colossians 3:1–4).
- Choose to live out of the 'tree of life." This is where there is life and freedom. The "tree of the knowledge of good and evil" is the death walk of religion. Religion always ends up with people *walking the plank.*
- Shame is an attack on your identity. Wear the CROWN and never let the accuser put you down. You can't have a better identity than the identity and life of Jesus within you (Galatians 2:20). You are a true child of the one true King! You are royalty!
- Think about your glorious future often.
- Satan is the "accuser of the brothers" (Revelation 12:10). Be careful to not intentionally or unintentionally attack the identity of your brother in Christ.

Fool's Gold:

- Religion, rules, and rituals don't make for better people.
- Hard work can be a good thing, but if it is a "God thing," then it becomes a bad thing. (Even work can become an idol.)
- "Fake it to make it!" This never works. You can't be right if you are not real. You can't be real if you are not right with God.
- The "self-made" man. Beware of pirates! No truly good man is self-made. Know this: "If you see a turtle sitting on a fence post, it didn't get there by itself!"
- Outward appearance; this is what most people dwell on. (God looks to the heart, 1 Samuel 16:7.)
- A life without scars. Think about it (James 1:1–3; Romans 5:3–6)! Let your scars become a "badge of honor."
- Letting feelings and accusations occupy your mind (Colossians 3:1–4). (Your soul will always be messed up, your mind, will, and emotions. Your mind can easily be confused; your will can have its flame doused, and your emotions can filibuster and *scupper* you.)
- Dwelling on the past. (Losers always tell people how good they were. Live in the present, with your hopes set on your glorious future)
- Always *hornswaggle*. (This way you will never be trusted, and you will always be on *chase,* and being chased.)

BASK: Wisdom

- Know this, bad captains will say: "The beatings will cease when morale improves." This is how it is on pirate ships. You are not a pirate. (Taken from a poster on a pirate ship.)

4.

The Hummingbird

Papa was down at the Rio Cobre River to fish. In reality, he was there to relax, and fishing was an excuse to sit by this beautiful river and enjoy God in His wonderful creation. As he threw his third line into the river over his shoulder, he saw Reo coming toward him, and he wasn't smiling today. Papa wasn't surprised to see Reo, and he wasn't surprised to see his foul mood, as Satan always tries to snatch the good seed. Sure, Papa hoped that Reo's heart would have been filled with hope and the joy of the Lord, but it wasn't; it was tainted with doubt and despair. The "little pirate" in him was trying to convince him to run, to chase, and to be a *freebooter* again. Papa was willing to listen, but he was trusting that he had enough cred with Reo to speak wisdom into his life.

They greeted each other cordially, and then Reo sat down and began to toss rocks into the river right by Papa's fishing line. Papa nudged Reo and asked, "What, were you raised on a pirate ship? You don't know much about fishing." Reo says, "As a matter of fact, I was." He then shook his head, apologized, and slumped his shoulders. Reo mumbled, "I've come here to let you know that I have decided to head back to sailing the seas." Papa asked, "Why would you want to be a *sea dog* again?" Reo was *addled*, but spoke up, "I just don't feel that I belong here." Reo laughed and condescendingly said, "So you don't feel like you belong, *aye?*" Papa offered an affirming nod and said, "*Sí.*" Papa just sat there and shook his head in disgust.

After a moment of silence, Papa offered, "So you don't 'feel' like farming; so you don't 'feel' the love here?" Reo responded in haste, "I feel the love, but *landlubbing* is like the *doldrums*: There is no adventure in it. It is dig, plant, and wait. I don't think it is for me, and I don't think I will ever feel like I belong. Don't get me wrong; you have good folks here, but they just don't understand me." Papa retorted, "So you don't 'feel' like you want to stay here. Do you really know what is going on in your soul?" Reo shook his head and said, "There you go again with that religious stuff. What is my soul?" Papa smiled and dug deeper, "You haven't had time to even get to know your own soul." Reo said, "I only came to see you out of respect. I don't want to be preached at. I didn't just want to run. I wanted to be good to you." Papa had appreciation in his eyes and said, "Thanks, but before

The Hummingbird

you go, let's have a talk. What do you say we head for the mahogany tree and have some sweet tea?" Reo opined, "Sounds good, but don't try to get me to stay." Papa said, "I learned a long time ago that a man convinced against his will is of the same opinion still." I only want you to stay if you want to stay. Everyone who is here at Shalom has this freedom. No one is forced into anything. We are not a religious community; we are a life-giving spiritually enriching family."

As they walked back to Shalom, both Papa and Reo could feel the joy all over the property. Children were playing on the swings under the trees. Earl was working his horses out in the fields, and they looked like they were smiling and having fun while at work. The women were baking and the smells were inviting. They had an audience out back with some of the invalids who found work peeling potatoes and canning vegetables. The laundry was blowing in the soft Jamaican breeze, and several workers were making their way back to the house for the midday siesta. There were joyful greetings abounding as Papa and Reo passed the people on their way to the mahogany tree.

After they sat down, they stayed quiet for a while and just gazed at the property, and out to the ocean which could be seen even, though it was a few miles away. There was a ship with its sails full of wind looking alive and free out there. Reo commented, "That looks so nice." Papa said, "You don't feel that you belong here?" Reo affirmed and said, "That is what I said." Papa asked, "Do you always live by feelings?" Reo asked, "What else do I have to go on?" Papa asked, "If you were sailing at night and saw a light from a lighthouse, what would you do? Go by feelings?" Reo answered, "No, I'd wait to see where we were, take some soundings, and then proceed with caution." Papa said, "I thought so. A Christian doesn't live by feelings; we are to live by faith."

Reo took a big breath, gathered himself, and said, "So, what do you do with the feelings?" Papa laughed and said, "Sometimes you have to tell them to shut up. Sometimes you have to tell them to go to hell, or to 'Be gone, Satan.'" Reo had never heard Papa talk so forcefully, and he was jolted. Gathering himself, he retorted, "*Shiver me timbers!* You are a real human being. Why so strong?" "The believer in Jesus must learn to rely on God's trustworthy Word, the witness of the Spirit, and reliable counsel—not our feelings. Our feelings are often tainted by the little pirate, our flesh, circumstances, Satan, and the world we live in." Reo laughed and said, "There you go again, talking about the little pirate. I don't get it."

Papa asked, "Will you let me explain?" Reo said, "What the *bilge,* go for it." Papa took dead aim like a fisherman with a harpoon, "I think you want to go back to the sea because that is what you know, and that is what you are comfortable doing. It feels better to you, and you probably feel more respected there because you know how to navigate a ship." Reo nodded, smiled, chuckled, and said, "*Sí, sí.* This is true." Papa then asked, "But what has God called you to?" Reo, with a frown on his face, hung his head and grumbled, "I really don't know." Papa said, "Pirates always *chase* when they don't know what else to do. It is what they do. You always swam to freedom; you risked; you revolted; you took action and sailed away." Reo smiled and said, "Sounds *corsair*, don't it?" Papa said, "It sounds like you are letting the little pirate, your flesh, run your life. The flesh is your 'old way' of doing things. It is the way you used to meet your needs, and you went that way because you made it work for you, or at least you thought it did."

Reo was defensive, "It worked and I felt alive and free." Papa said, "You call being sentenced to die by hanging being alive and free?" Reo stuttered, "It is what I knew." Papa said, "And you lived a very confused life as 'Red-Legs' Greaves." Reo asked, "How did you know?" Papa said, "I saw you when you were led in chains to the Port Royal Prison. I had heard the stories. I don't believe everything I hear, but I tell you the truth, if you want to live a long life, it won't be out terrorizing on the seas. There is a bounty on your head. Some pirate would like to make a name for himself, just like you made a name for yourself taking down Captain Hawkins."

Reo was quiet. Papa, after a moment of contemplation, said, "Jesus' disciples didn't have an easy life, either. This was a time when following Him was tough, and many ran away. But there was Peter who reckoned, "Where else can we go? Only you, Jesus, have the words of eternal life." I think you are in the same place." Reo asked, "But what about feeling like I belong?" Papa assured, "You are now among those who are called to belong to Jesus Christ. I assure you that you are accepted, just as you are in accepted in Christ by this community. You won't always feel like it, but you are accepted in the Beloved. If you believe this truth, it won't be long before you are experiencing God's joy in your life and fulfilling your true purpose. Is this the life you want?" Reo's eyes began to fill, and he said, "Yes, it is!" Papa asked, "Do you believe that Jesus Christ is your Lord and Savior? Do you know Him personally?" Reo said, "I haven't always lived for Him." Papa said, "I, too, used to live chasing performance-based acceptance, as a fish chases a shiny lure, thinking it would satisfy me and even make me right with God. It is not about what we do for Him. It is in believing what He has done for us by dying on the cross and rising again from the dead. Do you believe?" Reo answered strongly, "Yes, I believe in Jesus."

Papa rejoiced and said, "Reo, oftentimes good feelings will follow right beliefs. I believe this is one of those times." Reo affirmed and said, "Praise Jesus! Tell me why I wanted to *chase?*" Papa said, "You only know what you know; you are new to grace. Grace is something you don't earn. You are so used to living on the edge; you are used to pirating and taking from others. You were powered by adrenaline. You need to learn about the anointing. You are familiar with the *chase*; you will have to learn about contentment. You are familiar with being a *freebooter*; you need to accept your new family, and

The Hummingbird

they will accept you. You existed in a world dominated by fear. I invite you to let God love you because He does. His love will make you secure." Reo looked as if he had been hit broadside and said, "It is a new day for me." Papa smiled and hugged his head with his arm.

Papa asked, "We are sitting under this beautiful tree. May I tell you why I like it so much?" Reo said, "Yes, please." Papa said, "In God's garden, the Garden of Eden, there was the choice of two trees: the tree of life and the tree of the knowledge of good and evil. They chose the tree of the knowledge of good and evil. Ever since that time, people have been trying to earn love and acceptance by their good works. Living, but always being fearful that their knowledge of good things would outweigh the evil they had done. Yet, they were always reminded by the devil that they were in his religious tree and were doomed to die. Jesus died on the tree that was made into a cross, and by our faith in what was accomplished on that tree, we have been transferred out of the tree of the knowledge of good and evil into the tree of life. Here at Shalom we try to practice living out of the tree of life. We try not to bring up a person's past, and we will focus on our glorious future instead." Reo said, "That is a good thing. That is how I want to live because my past is so confusing."

As they were enjoying new freedom, they were feeling lighthearted, when they were gloriously interrupted by a red-billed streamertail hummingbird. This dazzling bird was flitting from flower to flower sucking nectar. It was amazing to see this little creature seemingly stand suspended in midair and even fly backwards while it did its work. Its iridescent green body—bright red bill with the black tip and its long tail—made this bird a beautiful and intriguing sight to behold. Papa and Reo enjoyed the show and realized that God was once again using His creation to affirm His work in their lives. As they began to discuss this beautiful visitor, Esther showed up with a tray of sugar cookies and a pitcher of sweet tea. They were happy to have the break. While enjoying the fellowship Papa asked Esther if she would sing the "Hummingbird" song they enjoyed so much. She was happy to oblige.

Beautiful Hummingbird, you wear a smile
Stay awhile

Beautiful Hummingbird, you defy nature's laws
Help us to pause

You are an inspiring creation
Beautiful and dutiful
Serving in our colorful garden

Beautiful Hummingbird, reflecting sunshine and glory
Your life tells a story

Stay with us, inspire us.
Don't fly away on your translucent wings
We enjoy you so much please stay

Beautiful Hummingbird, basking in sunshine
Drawing in sweetness, stay with us

The Hummingbird

Your chirp quickens our eyes
We look for you in the skies
Your stay with us delights us.

Beautiful Hummingbird, dazzling in flight
You remind us of God's might
Stay awhile

Gleaming and streaming illuminating space
Glorious rapture on each face

Beautiful Hummingbird, stay with us
Keep aloft and lift our hearts

You are pleasing we sense your essence.
Like an angel you are

Beautiful Hummingbird, work is effortless
you cause healthy, fragrant, growth,
Stay awhile

Stay and play, your dainty flight
Points us to abundant life

Beautiful Hummingbird, you make us smile
Our eyes become bright as you take flight
You catch the light
Stay awhile

You dance on the breeze, inspiring belief
Stay and play,
You are a portrait of grace

Beautiful Hummingbird, stay, stay,
Your green chest, a reason to flaunt
Your long black tail is a rudder and a sail
Stay awhile

Beautiful Hummingbird, where you go
We will never know,
Traverse the terrain
But please stay

Whirl, chatter, and sing
Beautiful Hummingbird
Our joy bells ring

Beautiful Hummingbird, please stay
Stay and play, we love to see you play,
Play all day.

The flowers are in bloom
We hope to see you soon.
When you can
Stay awhile

Papa and Reo applauded Esther for the beautiful way she sang this song. Esther gathered up the tray, the glasses, and the pitcher and headed to the plantation house. Reo reclined and said, "I've decided not to 'fly away.'" Papa rejoiced and said, "There is more to this song, this truth that we know. I believe you are called to be like the hummingbird." Reo shook his head and said, "And how am I to be like a hummingbird?" Papa opined, "These beautiful birds are great farmers; they work for

God and cause things to grow. I think you are to be like that." Reo responded with vigor, "*Yo-ho-ho,* I don't know, tell me more." Papa said, "Like the song said, he is a gardener; he causes beautiful things to grow; he brings a beautiful fragrance, but it takes understanding. He doesn't fly away; he stays and works. I can't believe how long he can stay in one place. Those little wings really whirl." Reo chuckled, "I have much to think about, but I won't fly away!"

Papa and Reo agree to take the time every day to discuss these spiritual lessons. Reo is grateful to have had Papa speak into his life.

The next day was Bible study night, and the group was eager to gather. After a delightful time of worshiping with songs and prayer, Tim got up and read Proverbs 4:1–27:

Security in Wisdom

1
Hear, *my* children, the instruction of a father,
And give attention to know understanding;
2
For I give you good doctrine:
Do not forsake my law.
3
When I was my father's son,
Tender and the only one in the sight of my mother,

4
He also taught me, and said to me:
"Let your heart retain my words;
Keep my commands, and live.
5
Get wisdom! Get understanding!
Do not forget, nor turn away from
the words of my mouth.
6
Do not forsake her, and she will preserve you;
Love her, and she will keep you.
7
Wisdom *is* the principal thing;
Therefore get wisdom.
And in all your getting, get understanding.
8
Exalt her, and she will promote you;
She will bring you honor, when you embrace her.
9
She will place on your head an ornament of grace;
A crown of glory she will deliver to you."
10
Hear, my son, and receive my sayings,
And the years of your life will be many.
11
I have taught you in the way of wisdom;
I have led you in right paths.
12
When you walk, your steps will not be hindered,
And when you run, you will not stumble.

13
Take firm hold of instruction, do not let go;
Keep her, for she *is* your life.
14
Do not enter the path of the wicked,
And do not walk in the way of evil.
15
Avoid it, do not travel on it;
Turn away from it and pass on.
16
For they do not sleep unless they have done evil;
And their sleep is taken away unless
they make *someone* fall.
17
For they eat the bread of wickedness,
And drink the wine of violence.
18
But the path of the just *is* like the shining sun,
That shines ever brighter unto the perfect day.
19
The way of the wicked *is* like darkness;
They do not know what makes them stumble.
20
My son, give attention to my words;
Incline your ear to my sayings.
21
Do not let them depart from your eyes;
Keep them in the midst of your heart;
22
For they *are* life to those who find them,
And health to all their flesh.

23
Keep your heart with all diligence,
For out of it *spring* the issues of life.
24
Put away from you a deceitful mouth,
And put perverse lips far from you.
25
Let your eyes look straight ahead,
And your eyelids look right before you.
26
Ponder the path of your feet,
And let all your ways be established.
27
Do not turn to the right or the left;
Remove your foot from evil.
(Proverbs 4:1–27)

Papa stood up and with clarity said, "This passage expresses a loving father's heart. A loving father wants you to 'get wisdom,' and 'get understanding.' Getting wisdom is the principal thing! Think about it: In our lives, there are lots of things we go to get! Therefore let's make the 'getting of wisdom' the most important 'get' we seek. If we live this way, we will be blessed as 'she'—wisdom is called a beautiful woman—wants to bless us. She will bless us with the right path; she will help us to not stumble. She will keep us from living like pirates. You know that they are into all types of wickedness: drunkenness, darkness, and violence."

Papa then led the congregation in a simple prayer, "Lord God, we ask you to help us to keep our hearts with all diligence, because we know that from our hearts spring forth the issues of life. Help us to flow in the river of your grace. Amen!"

The group appreciated this succinct lesson and prayer. Immediately Reo came forward and asked, "Did you make this lesson just for me?" They embraced and laughed together.

BASK: Wisdom

Gold Nuggets of Wisdom:

- The wise can spot a fool.
- Never despise wisdom; always seek for it as you would seek for gold.
- Always have a godly mentor in your life that you can bounce things off. There is wisdom in godly counsel.
- Stay away from fools! A companion of fools will be destroyed (Proverbs 13:20).
- A fool shows disrespect to authorities.
- Fools hate the truth and can't be trusted.
- A fool stays stiff-necked even when the facts are against him.
- A fool is anyone who loves things above God.
- Pirates are fools because they chase at the drop of a hat.
- Consequences should be a good teacher.
- A fool reveals everything he knows.
- A fool can't admit his mistakes.
- A fool brags about his cheating.
- True riches are being "rich in God."
- Anointing is the ability to live out of our true identity.
- Trust truth. Study to show yourself approved as a good workman analyzing the holy Scriptures (2 Timothy 2:15).
- Faith is taking God at His word and not relying on self (Hebrews 11:1,6).
- Life begins when we die to self, Satan, and this world.

- Always ask "what does God's Word say about this?"
- Knowing that we belong to Jesus is the key to contentment.
- Always *avast*.
- Know the TRUTH-TRUST-RELATIONSHIP-JOY continuum and learn to live the truth so that "feelings" won't always be tearing your sails.

BASK: Wisdom

Fool's Gold:

- Money is always the measure of success.
- Many fancy words (where there are many words, sin is not absent. Talk is cheap)!
- Winning the argument, but losing the relationship. (Value relationships; pirates cut bait and *sail on.*)
- Believing that "he who dies with the most toys is the winner."
- Believing what people say about you. (Only believe what God believes about you! Study His holy Word to know His thoughts about you.)
- The end justifies the means.
- Winning at all costs. (Some things are more valuable than winning.)
- Cheating your way to victory. (You know the truth and so does God!)
- Adrenaline is a purely fleshly and physical way to live.
- Fools live in the past. (God shapes us by our glorious future.)
- "Feeling" that you are on the right track.
- Being loved by people. (Can be a good thing, but if the people are pirates, it is a bad thing.) The "fear of man is a snare."
- Thinking that being busy is good. (Activity is not necessarily productivity.)
- Chasing shiny objects; they must be valuable! (Just because it is shiny doesn't mean it is valuable. Remember how monkey catchers trap

monkeys with shiny trinkets in glass jars. Pyrite looks shiny, but it is flaky and cheap.
- Being a freebooter—always looking for ways to *plunder* people.
- Being a mooch, never spending your own *loot*.
- *Chasing, Chasing, Chasing.* Filling your wings with adrenaline and your sails with greed. (Living this way will most certainly *maroon* you.)

5.

Earl's "Broken" Horses

Earl truly enjoys working with his horses. He finds many ways to use his horses around Shalom. He digs foundations for homes, trenches for planting sugar cane, and hauling stalks into town on his horse-drawn wagon. His favorite thing to do is giving the children rides on Onyx, his prized Belgian steed. Onyx stands tall and proud at 19 hands high. She weighs in at over 2,000 pounds of horse and can pull stumps out of the ground like you would pull a sliver out of your thumb.

Reo has taken to working with the horses. Of course his favorite is Onyx, but Earl is training him to work with Boaz and Samson—affectionately named after two of Earl's favorite Old Testament men. To get this team to respond, Earl uses loud and coarse language to get the horses to react to his various commands. Earl has little problem getting Reo to coax these animals with loud and forceful language because, as Earl says, "Reo is a natural," and his Scottish accent is a plus.

During a break, Earl tells Reo his salvation story. He admits that on the fateful day when Port Royal was plunged into the sea, if he had died in the tide, he believes he would be in hell today. He let Reo know that—while trying to pluck people out of the liquefied sand they were stuck in—he lost Ivory as the water backwashed up into the bank. Ivory was a beautiful partner to Onyx, a beautiful light-colored Belgian. As he is telling this story, Reo is struck with silence as he realizes that at the exact same time Onyx and Ivory were pulling people out of the mire, he was being splashed out of the Port Royal Prison and tossed into the bay by a mighty wave. He flashed back to his memory and remembered swimming out to the whaling ship, where they picked him up and gave him a fresh start and freedom. Reo has been daydreaming about this new "fresh start" that he is able to enjoy by the grace of God. Earl catches Reo not paying attention to him and asks, "Are you *blaggarding* me?" Reo quickly apologizes by saying, "I am sorry, brother; I was just taken back to what that day was like for everyone." Earl is happy and is enjoying this captive audience even though he is a man of few words. It is amazing that a man who rarely said a word, now gushes with enthusiasm when he talks about Jesus and his faith in Him. He says, "I think God used that day to reach me. I was an ornery old cuss before I got saved. Think of it: God used me to save lots of people that day. Tim and Papa had me get the steeds hitched up quickly, and with a long rope, we plucked many people out of the sea. It was swallowing them up like the big fish swallowed Jonah. God used that day to save me. Think of it: I was being used to save people, but God used the tragedy to save me!" Reo was now caught up in the story and asked, "How did God use a tragedy like that to save you?"

Earl laughed and said, "I have worked with horses my whole life. I love them, but you would not have known it by the way I yelled at them. I used every cuss word known to man to coax them into obeying me. But when I witnessed Port Royal, that wicked city sinking into the sea, I realized that I deserved to go down with it. I was a bad man. By God's grace, I started listening to Papa, Tim, Clay, Chase, and Nick. My conversations with them inspired me to believe in Jesus. I also think the beautiful music from Esther got ahold of my heart. I think I got saved just like a horse gets broken." Reo asked, "What is a 'broken horse'?"

Earl chuckled, and then said, "A broken horse is a good horse; I know that sounds odd, but it is true. Unless a horse has its wild spirit broken, it is good for nothing. They are not useful. But, a broken horse will listen, obey, and work for you. It will then become a delightful friend. That earthquake and the aftermath broke me, man. You should have seen the death and the devastation. It got to me." Reo asked, "Explain what a broken horse is again; how does it happen?" Earl joked, "You been out at sea your whole life?" Reo said, "*Aye,* and I've been with pirates more than horses." Earl nodded, saying, "*Arrrr,* I get it. You haven't seen a bronc rider break a horse, have you, *matey!*"

Looking at Boaz and Samson, Earl spits and says, "See these beautiful steeds? When they were young, they were a handful. They were beautiful, yes, and playful, but neither wanted to bridle up or take a saddle. Wild like that they were good for 'nutin'; they had to be broken first. They were like pirates who just did whatever they wanted to do—*Yo-ho-ho*—and they would chase, fight, raid, pillage, rape, and rebel at every whim. So we had to break them." Reo looked more confused than ever, so he asked, "Are you talking about horses or pirates?" Earl said, "*Arrrr,* both!" Then Earl pointed him to the corral where some young bucks had a young horse on the rope; it was kicking and pulling, trying to break free. They walked to the training area, grabbed some long strands of grass growing next to a post, and as they leaned on the fence, each had a strand of grass in their mouth. As they chewed on the grass, they watched some buckaroos go about "breaking" Moses, a wild young horse. Reo commented, "This is the best show I have seen in a while." The young buckaroos kept getting bucked off Moses.

Earl explained, "Each rider will saddle-up and try to ride the horse. The young steed will try to buck him off; see why they are called 'buckaroos'?" Reo was fully engrossed in this process. Enamored with the efforts of the young men, they cheered as they began to have some success. He asked, "Why do they keep getting on the horse when it is going to buck them off again and again? It is like *kissing the gunner's daughter!*" Earl laughed, "*Sink me,* you get it. They have to keep getting back on. That is why there are three of them. When one gets bucked off, the other is there to get on; they will keep trying to ride him till he surrenders, or till the horse is broken." Reo said, "What do you mean by broken?"

"*Shiver me timbers,* Earl shouted, "you don't get it, do you? Those buckaroos are going to ride that horse until it decides to cooperate. And when it does, it is a beautiful thing." Reo, paying attention to the horse, said, "It has got to be worn out. I'd be spittin' mad." Earl said, "And that is what has to get broken out of the steed. He has to decide that it is better to obey, better to get along, and better to respond to the rider than to buck him off. He has to *want* to get along with the rider." They stayed at the fence for a good while. It was starting to get hot, and the riders were hoping the horse would come to its senses before they had to go for the shade and siesta. Sure enough, the miracle happened: Moses quit bucking; he calmed down, snorted, smiled, and began to respond to the simple commands of the buckaroos. They gave him some sugar and hay, and it became compliant. He was like a completely different horse. He became responsive, cooperative, and pleasant.

Earl explained, "I think Moses is getting the message. Later today they will see if he is broken; if not, they will go through the whole process again. But, if he is broken, Moses could be a good animal. He could plow, pull a wagon, and even ride the range. He will be useful. He is a beauty, but unless he is broken, he is no good." Reo asked, "What do you look for in a good horse?" Earl answered, "He has to be broken; he has to respond to my voice; he has to be willing to obey; he has to want to be with me. I am really looking for a friend. I need to be able to trust him, and he needs to trust me. It is really a relationship, and when you have it, it is quite special. A good horse can be the best friend you ever have." Reo nodded his head and headed for a hammock under the shade trees. From this perch he could see the sea, the farm, and Shalom, their home.

While lying back in the hammock, Reo pulled his straw hat over his eyes and began to reflect. He couldn't help but think about the Port Royal earthquake. He imagined seeing Earl there with Onyx and Ivory—his great Belgian steeds—pulling people out of the liquefied sand, saving lives. Thinking about Ivory getting caught in the undertow of the tidal wave and being tossed and drowned in the bay gave him a painful pause. In his daydream, he saw himself, in the exact same undercurrent, being washed out of the prison, plunged beneath the debris and safely squirted out into the middle of the bay. He couldn't help but believe it was God's hand saving him and helping him swim to safety. This rescue was nothing of his made-up imagination or effort. He was awed by the realization that the whaling ship just happened to be there when he needed to be saved, and the crew was happy to save him. He just knew it was God who orchestrated this great rescue. He just knew it had something to do with God's grace and God's call on his life.

After a light dinner, Earl approached Reo to see if he wanted to visit the corral and see how Moses was doing. Reo said, "Shoot-fire, boy, howdy, guns 'a blazin,' I am all in." Earl answered, "I'll take that as *Aye!*" When they got to the corral, Moses was happy to greet them. He, too, had enjoyed the time of siesta—and his strength was back—but his spirit was one with the men. Earl and Reo watered them and fed them hay and sugar cubes, and Moses allowed them to easily bridle him up. With the rope to the bridle, Reo enjoyed walking Moses around the corral, while Earl reminded him constantly to talk to him and to let him recognize his voice.

After a while of walking, the buckaroos returned to see if they needed another session. Upon seeing the buckaroos, Moses bristled and riled up a bit, but then quickly settled down. He allowed them to slowly put on a small English saddle on, and soon a buckaroo was riding and teaching Moses some simple commands. Reo stood there at the fence rail amazed and realized that brokenness had turned Moses into a different and better animal. Earl realized that he didn't have to talk much because the proof of authentic brokenness was in the pudding. Moses was becoming a better and purposeful animal.

They went to a bench and sat and watched the young buckaroo put Moses through the paces. Earl explained the training process to Reo, and Reo nodded his understanding. Earl commented, "Wisdom is all about understanding, isn't it!" Reo agreed and then asked, "Tell me how God breaks us?" Earl let out a big smile then said, "You know, I don't know the Bible like Papa, but this is what I learned. I think God breaks us like these buckaroos break a horse. Papa, he had me batten down this passage from Matthew 5 called the Sermon on the Mount. Jesus said":

3
"Blessed *are* the poor in spirit,
For theirs is the kingdom of heaven.
4
"Blessed *are* those who mourn,
For they shall be comforted.
5
"Blessed *are* the meek,
For they shall inherit the earth."
(Matthew 5:3–5)

"I know this doesn't sound like horse talk, but it is. When Jesus said 'blessed are the meek,' He was thinking about a strong horse like Onyx, so don't think that meek means weak. It doesn't; it means 'power under control.' But to get to this blessed place of power under control, we all have to become 'poor in spirit.' That is the opposite of being rich in pride. *Sí, sí,* the proud man lives like he doesn't need God. He is like the pirate and is totally self-dependent and intent on meeting his own needs. The humble man is a man who realizes he needs God. When that earthquake happened, it was over. I knew I needed God." Reo broke in, "I look back and realize that is when I realized I didn't save myself. If it weren't for God, I wouldn't be here."

Earl agreed and then said, "Pride shows up in our lives in the '9 P's' of identity idolatry. I don't know if Papa has taught you this yet, but he will. The 'P's' are all rooted in pride. They are Position-Power, Prestige, Popularity, Possessions, Physical appearance, Pleasure, Performance, Philosophy, and the Past. If you can understand these idols and confront your pride, you will be humble; you will be like Moses, when he got broken."

Reo shook his head in disgust, "I think you just described my life. I coveted all of those characteristics, but now I see that they are truly pirate-like." Earl was full of joy and said, "This is a good thing. This shows that you are now poor in spirit, and now yours is the kingdom of God." Reo was emphatic, "I never knew that this was the tell." Earl asked, "What is a tell?" Reo said, "When pirates play cards, they always have a manner about them that gives away what cards they are holding in their hand."

Earl said, "I get it. I've seen men playing cards and even dice. Listen to this Scripture from Isaiah 66:2: 'But on this *one* will I look: On *him who is* poor and of a contrite spirit, And who trembles at My word.'"

"Isaiah, a prophet of God, said that, and it is true: Like the horse, we are only useful when we realize we need Him for everything. Being 'poor in spirit' is the opposite of being 'rich' in pride. Pirates are rich in pride and act like they don't need God. Let me explain. King Solomon said":

2
Every way of a man *is* right in his own eyes,
But the LORD weighs the hearts.
3
To do righteousness and justice
Is more acceptable to the LORD than sacrifice.
4
A haughty look, a proud heart,
And the plowing of the wicked *are* sin.
(Proverbs 21:2-4)

"I think the pirate way is a proud and haughty way. You know how they esteem the *swagger* of the *swashbuckler!*" Reo chuckled and said, "Their pride makes them *bungholes.*" Earl nodded his agreement and retorted, "They will all end up *feeding the fish*. Pride is a terrible affront to God. I had to deal with this in my life, and I hid this Proverb in my heart. Listen":

2
When pride comes, then comes shame;
But with the humble *is* wisdom.

3
The integrity of the upright will guide them,
But the perversity of the unfaithful will destroy them.
4
Riches do not profit in the day of wrath,
But righteousness delivers from death.
(Proverbs 11:2-4)

Clay and Tim were always visiting the stable and helping out with the horses and the implements because they could fix things in the blacksmith shop. Clay leaned up against the fence, and Tim took a seat on the bench. They both delighted in sharing in this godly spiritual conversation. This discussion about humility and brokenness was encouraging and inspiring to the men. Clay was exuberant and asked if he could share a favorite song with them about this matter, so there under the Jamaican sky with the cool dusky evening moving in, he sang "Channels Only":

How I praise Thee precious Savior,
that Thy love laid hold of me;
Thou hast saved and cleansed and filled me
That I might Thy channel be.

Channels only, Blessed Master,
But with all Thy wondrous pow'r
Flowing through us, Thou canst use us
Ev'ry day and ev'ry hour.

BASK: Wisdom

> *Emptied that Thou shouldest fill me,*
> *A clean vessel in Thy hand;*
> *With no pow'r but as Thou givest*
> *Graciously with each command.*
>
> *Channels only, Blessed Master,*
> *But with all Thy wondrous pow'r*
> *Flowing through us, Thou canst use us*
> *Ev'ry day and ev'ry hour.*
>
> *Witnessing Thy pow'r to save me,*
> *Setting free from self and sin,*
> *Thou who broughtest to possess me,*
> *In Thy fullness, Lord, come in.*
>
> *Channels only, Blessed Master,*
> *But with all Thy wondrous pow'r*
> *Flowing through us, Thou canst use us*
> *Ev'ry day and ev'ry hour.*
>
> *Jesus, fill now with Thy Spirit*
> *Hearts that full surrender know,*
> *That the streams of living water*
> *From our inner man may flow.*
>
> *Channels only, Blessed Master,*
> *But with all Thy wondrous pow'r*
> *Flowing through us, Thou canst use us*
> *Every day and every hour.*

Reo was grateful to have these sincere friends and told them so. Being unprovoked, Earl went out in the corral, and Moses came to him. Earl then took Moses to Reo and said, "Brother, I would like to introduce you to your horse." Reo asked, "Are you sure?" Earl said, "For real." Tim and Clay all laughed. Tim said, "You have lots of work to do." All Reo could say was, 'Thank you, thank you. I have never been given such a gift." Tim said, "Thankfulness is the key to everything. I have heard that before, and it is true." Reo was humbled and felt like he belonged at Shalom. He hugged Moses' neck, and the two of them went for a long walk together.

BASK: Wisdom

Gold Nuggets of Wisdom:

- With humility comes wisdom.
- Be humble enough to seek out godly mentors.
- "True humility and fear of the LORD leads to riches, honor, and long life" (Proverbs 22:4).
- Let your good conscience keep you humble and let it be a good guide for you.
- With humility, even your weaknesses can become your strengths (think about it).
- Your failures are not fatal; they can lead you to true humility, and then they become your entrance into other people's lives.
- Humility will allow you to ask smarter and more experienced people for their help and their insights.
- Be humble and ask for help and directions. (Remember the children of Israel wandered for 40 years because they didn't ask for directions.)
- Realize that there are no "little people"; everyone matters to God.
- Never give the air that you are too good for anybody or too proud to do honest work, no matter how dirty it is.
- Learn to let God break you quickly. Don't fight Him. The sooner you let Him have you entirely, the better your life will be.
- You can let God have you because He is holy, trustworthy, and loving.
- Become familiar with the "9 P's" of *identity idolatry* and let God purge them from your life.

Fool's Gold:

- "Fake it to make it."
- Focus on appearance; just judge the book by its cover.
- Have a form of godliness.
- Have a "losers limp."
- Make excuses.
- Be a victim.
- Act entitled.
- Expect others to bail your water.
- Have loud thunder, but no rain.
- Don't ever show your weakness; bluff like you are only strong.
- Covet and lust after other people's stuff.
- Act and live like you don't need God. Act like you have it all together.
- Develop a pirate *swagger and strut.*
- Show off all your treasures. Have a gold earring. (These were to provide pirates with a proper burial.)
- Brag about your conquests and be sure to let your pride show.
- Be rich in pride.

6.

Pirates Are Liars, Perverted, and Bound

Now that Jesus had become Christina's Lord and Savior, she has become a beautiful woman in every way. As a teenager, she was swept up off the streets in London and shipped to Port Royal, where she was expected to serve the sailing men in the sex trade. This is not what she wanted to do with her life. In reality she didn't know what she was to do with her life. On the day Port Royal sank into the sea, she was pulled safely out of the quicksand. On a personal level, she was aimless and adrift in a sea of filth. Literally she was a person who was tossed to-and-fro by the waves of uncertainty and insecurity.

In London she had no family, no morals, no one to be accountable to, no one who cared for her, no hopeful future, and no sense of who she really was. When the agents of the courts interviewed her, she was so aimless they hurried her off to the port and had her labeled to work in the sex trade, serving the sexually starved men in Port Royal, the most wicked city in the world. The Madam met her and showed her some seductive skills. To her surprise, she made *booty;* she used her *booty* to make *booty.* Being forced to work in the sex trade was the only way she knew how to make *loot.* She never liked what she did. It became who she was, and in a creepy way, she enjoyed being desired and prized by men, even though they just wanted to use her to satisfy their wanton appetites. To stomach this lifestyle, she allowed her conscience to be seared, and she became emotionally numb to the immorality of her craft. Her only real concern was for her survival because the pirates she met would say nice things to her, but only to get her to serve them. She knew they were takers only and had nothing to offer her, except some *pieces of eight.*

Christina loved her newfound freedom and her new life as a child of God. Being mentored by Esther and Wyndolyn was imparting to her a purpose that made her feel like the richest person in Spanish Town. She was beginning to understand what love is and was learning to apply wisdom to her life. She was Esther and Wyndolyn's joy and crown.

Her problem is her beauty, and the men are smitten by her and would like for her to be their trophy. What she doesn't understand is that she, too, enjoys being desired and doesn't know she is a natural flirt. The men are always attracted to her; she has that seductive look that says "come and get me," yet she acts like she has nothing to do with it. She really doesn't want to have sex with men. She wants healthy relationships, but doesn't know how to make them grow. But, her naïveté is cause for some mixed-up messages. Reo is flat out desirous of her, but doesn't know how to act around her. It is a good thing that he has a horse to train, because left unbridled, he would be chasing Christina for all the wrong reasons.

The past is beginning to catch up with Reo. He, too, has a sexual history. He savored pulling into port with pockets full of silver and gold and the women hanging out of the whorehouse windows clamoring for his attention. He, too, had the *swagger*, and the plaid kilt was his moniker. He was always eager to *splice the main brace*; like all sailing men, they always acted like they deserved to be pleasured after sailing the rough and boisterous seas. As a captain, he lived as if he were entitled to the best and the most beautiful when it came to women. This was his past, but it was catching up to him. He and Christina are like fire when they are together. Or should we say, she adds fire to his burning flame? Their old ways were bringing the "little pirate" out of them as they got in the habit of meeting out under the stars. They loved to watch the water splash up on to the beach, and they liked how they could get each other sexually aroused. They were becoming a *bung* of emotions, and they were talking themselves in to *hornswaggling* each other sexually. Shoot-fire, they wanted each other and were justifying their thoughts—that is until Papa had a sit-down conversation with Reo and Esther, and Wyndolyn caught up with Christina in the kitchen.

Christina and Reo got caught with their hands in the cookie jar walking into Shalom in the wee hours of the morning. No one had been checking in on them. They had been treated like responsible adults, but now their brothers and sisters had to act like their "brother's keeper" and have a talk. Papa wasn't surprised; after all, this was Reo's lifestyle prior to coming to Shalom. Now that he was alive in the faith, he needed to learn the ways of the Lord. Papa was counting on the Holy Spirit to convict and to help in the transformation process. Even though he needed to be firm and disciplined, he didn't want to bring the "law of condemnation" that would only incite rebellion. Papa went to the corral where he was sure to find Reo working with Moses. At the fence, he broached the subject and asked Reo to meet him under the mahogany tree for a conversation.

Reo had never had a man speak morality into his life. Life on pirate ships was a free-for-all, and everyone played grab-ass all the time. From his experience, it was all about conquest and getting all you could while you had a chance. It was about adrenaline and the chase. Little did he know that Papa knew all about a man's ways, and he knew how to use the Bible to speak to these issues of the heart. Papa had put himself into a good frame of mind because he didn't want Reo to run away. He just wanted to show him the more excellent way.

Reo—with his hat in his hand and his face downcast—approached Papa sitting under the mahogany tree, positioned in a chair with sweet tea ready to serve Reo. After a cordial greeting, Papa asked Reo if he would like some tea, and Reo affirmed how good that would be after working with Moses in the corral. Then Papa got right to the point saying, "Reo, I know that you have been sneaking out with Christina late at night, and in the dark, you have been meeting with her. Why do you think I want to talk with you about this?" Reo was perplexed and said, "I really don't know. I thought I was free to do as I pleased." Papa chuckled and said, "Yes, you are free, and that is why I am talking with you. I don't want you to be doing things that would take away your freedom, or Christina's freedom. The enemy of our souls wants to see you in bondage, and that is why I am talking with you. It really is about freedom, but be careful not to use your Christian liberty as an excuse to indulge your flesh, you know, the little pirate. It is about freedom, but it is also about respect: respect for God, His Word, and for Christina."

Reo laughed, smiled and said, "Papa, do you know who I am? Do you know that I was 'Red-Legs' Greaves? I was the Scottish sailing man who wore the colorful plaid Scottish kilt. That is how I got the name Red-Legs, and when I would pull into port, I had my way with the ladies. They were always happy to see me, and I made them feel good about being with me. I had my way; I had the *swag and the swagger.*" Papa shook his head in disgust and said, "I know who you *were*—I just want to know who you *are*. I want to see you finding true freedom by living out of your true identity in Jesus." Reo stuttered and asked, "How does taking time with Christina keep me from freedom?" Papa answered, "If you are engaged sexually, it is like a drug. Sexual thoughts can consume your life and control you. They have a way of *scuppering* wholesome thinking and turning you into a pirate that will throw your prey overboard and *maroon* them. You see, it is not just about you. Christina is your sister in Christ, and we want to see that she is treated like a princess. Do you know about her previous life?"

Reo was silent and stammered, "I have never looked at it that way before. I guess I have been like a pirate, even though I have fought that image my whole life." Papa said, "Red, I believe you are a new man, but you need to learn the new ways you are to live, so you can walk in newness of life. It is a life of freedom and grace. I didn't come to condemn you; I just want to help you. Will you let me teach you some of these new ways?" Red said, "Shoot fire, fire away. I want to learn." Papa said, "Great, a disciple of Jesus is really a learner, and we are all in the process of growth. First of all, I want you to know that you are free to develop a relationship with Christina. I just want you to love and respect her." Red affirmed his agreement by nodding his head. Papa continued, "Get to know her story, know her heart, and don't do things under the cloak of darkness. God wants you to walk in the light. Light is your true identity! I know that the enemy uses darkness, so don't give him that opportunity. So, walk in the light, and learn the ways of the Lord. Do you know that pornography, promiscuity, and adultery are traps?" Red answered, "I don't even know what those big words mean." Papa said, "Let me begin by teaching you out of Proverbs, chapter five. You will see that your chaste behavior is very important to God."

Papa read from the sheets of Scripture that he brought with him:

The Peril of Adultery

1
My son, pay attention to my wisdom;
Lend your ear to my understanding,

2
That you may preserve discretion,
And your lips may keep knowledge.

3
For the lips of an immoral woman drip honey,
And her mouth *is* smoother than oil;

4
But in the end she is bitter as wormwood,
Sharp as a two-edged sword.

5
Her feet go down to death,
Her steps lay hold of hell.

6
Lest you ponder *her* path of life—
Her ways are unstable;
You do not know *them.*

7
Therefore hear me now, *my* children,
And do not depart from the words of my mouth.
8
Remove your way far from her,
And do not go near the door of her house,
9
Lest you give your honor to others,
And your years to the cruel *one;*
10
Lest aliens be filled with your wealth,
And your labors *go* to the house of a foreigner;
11
And you mourn at last,
When your flesh and your body are consumed,
12
And say:
"How I have hated instruction,
And my heart despised correction!
13
I have not obeyed the voice of my teachers,
Nor inclined my ear to those who instructed me!
14
I was on the verge of total ruin,
In the midst of the assembly and congregation."
15
Drink water from your own cistern,
And running water from your own well.
16
Should your fountains be dispersed abroad,
Streams of water in the streets?

17
Let them be only your own,
And not for strangers with you.
18
Let your fountain be blessed,
And rejoice with the wife of your youth.
19
As a loving deer and a graceful doe,
Let her breasts satisfy you at all times;
And always be enraptured with her love.
20
For why should you, my son, be
enraptured by an immoral woman,
And be embraced in the arms of a seductress?
21
For the ways of man are before the eyes of the LORD,
And He ponders all his paths.
22
His own iniquities entrap the wicked man,
And he is caught in the cords of his sin.
23
He shall die for lack of instruction,
And in the greatness of his folly he shall go astray.
(Proverbs 5:1–23)

Papa took some time to explain these thoughts to Red. Red was pleased to learn these truths and blunderstruck to realize that the Bible spoke to this topic so clearly. They agreed to get together again tomorrow and have more study time on this subject. They prayed together, and Red felt corrected, but he also felt loved.

Esther and Wyndolyn at the same time were meeting with Christina on the back steps of the outdoor kitchen. They took some time to express their love and concern to Christina, but Christina thought she was about to be scolded, so naturally she began to clam up and sulk. Esther and Wyndolyn tried to explain that men are known to give a little love to get sex, while women think that they can give a little sex to get love. Esther asked, "Christina, what do you want? Do you want sex, or do you want love? The two are not the same." With teardrops forming under her big brown eyes and running next to her nose, trembling with a tense face, she said, "I want love. What do you think? I don't want to be regarded as a floozy or a whore." Esther and Wyndolyn spontaneously chimed, "We had no doubt." Then Esther said, "You are not a whore. We want to help you wear the CROWN, be the princess you really are, and get the prince who will love you with the love of the Lord." The three of them embraced, then Esther asked, "May we share a Proverb with you?" Quietly Christine nodded affirmatively, as Esther read:

Beware of Adultery

20
My son, keep your father's command,
And do not forsake the law of your mother.

21
Bind them continually upon your heart;
Tie them around your neck.
22
When you roam, they will lead you;
When you sleep, they will keep you;
And *when* you awake, they will speak with you.
23
For the commandment *is* a lamp,
And the law a light;
Reproofs of instruction *are* the way of life,
24
To keep you from the evil woman,
From the flattering tongue of a seductress.
25
Do not lust after her beauty in your heart,
Nor let her allure you with her eyelids.
26
For by means of a harlot
A man is reduced to a crust of bread;
And an adulteress will prey upon his precious life.
27
Can a man take fire to his bosom,
And his clothes not be burned?
28
Can one walk on hot coals,
And his feet not be seared?
29
So *is* he who goes in to his neighbor's wife;
Whoever touches her shall not be innocent.
(Proverbs 6:20–29)

After hearing this passage, Christina was put off and put up a defensive emotional wall. Wyndolyn asked, "Why do you bristle at this?" Christina exclaimed, "I am not an 'evil woman.' I am not an adulteress." Esther affirmed, "We know that you are not; you are a holy child of God. But we need to understand God's commands, so that we can have the love in our lives that He wants for us." Christina nodded and asked, "Tell me more." Esther replied, "This Proverb gives some good guidance. We need to learn not to lead a man on with our words. We don't want to be seductive." Christina asked, "What does that mean?" Wyndolyn explained, "We don't want to lure a man to us as if we are bait for a fish. We want them to pursue us for the right reasons. Make him wait. Play hard-to-get. Know that you are worth it. So, be modest." Once again Christina asked, "What does it mean to be modest?" Esther answered, "Modesty is an attitude and a way of covering yourself. Men get turned on sexually by what they see, but we don't want them to want us for our flesh. We want them to value us as precious people."

Christina was beginning to open up and stated, "I have never had a woman speak to me like this. I was instructed by the Madam how to tease and attract sex business. It really messed me up."

Esther said, "That is your past. God has a beautiful life for you, but you must not be in the dark. I mean *literally* keep your relationship with Reo in the light. I don't think you should be with him in darkness. Make him get to know you and talk with you in the light.

Make him decide not to be pirate-like in his behavior. You know they dine and dash, hit and run, get their sex and go, *yo-ho-ho!* See if he really desires a relationship, and if that is what he wants, you can begin to build a relationship. Most men are afraid of intimacy. See if he is a real man who will value a real relationship." Christina smiled and said, "I think I get it." The ladies embraced and prayed.

A few days went by. Reo—who now was going by his real name Red—spent most of his time helping with the farming and working with Moses in the corral. He spent this time thinking about what Papa talked with him about and went by the kitchen to see Christina. They had a nice conversation and agreed to meet Wednesday evening for the Bible study. Later in the day, Papa came by the corral. Red thanked him for the counsel he had received and asked, "Why is it that I want sex like I do?" Papa laughed and said, "Maybe it is because you are a man, and God made you this way. Come over to the tree and I will try to explain." Red said, "Let me feed and water Moses, and I will be right there." When Red arrived, Papa offered him some sweet tea and jumped right in to the conversation. "Red, I think God made sex to be good. After all, He is holy, but Satan came along and tried to muddy the waters. You asked why we as men are so driven to chase sex. I think it is because of the little pirate in us who acts like a pirate. It is as simple as dice, splice, trice, and spice." Red rolled his eyes, chuckled, and said, "What, dice and splice what?" Papa said, "You know the words. Pirates live by adrenaline: They love the thrills of gambling, of hitting and running, and they love to roll the dice. If they don't value the relationship with a woman, it is all about the thrill." Red was nodding his head and said, "Yes, it is." Then Papa explained, "You remember being out at sea for a month or so and as soon as your ship landed, you were ready to *splice the main brace.* Any excuse was an excuse to reward yourself with pleasure. Some chased down the rum, others the women, but most did both." Red laughed heartily and said, "Yeah, whatever we did, we felt entitled to get lathered up. It was why we did it. Rum and sex were our rewards. What are the other words or reasons for sex?"

Papa was inspired, saying, "You know these ideas came from Chase. He used these words to help Tim understand this obsession. The next word he coined is "trice." As you know, a trice is a hoist device to lift cargo out of the *bilge* of the ship. Chase reasoned that men like to "hoist" up their egos, and sex can make a man feel big. The other word is "spice," and it stands to reason because no one likes dull, boring food. Sometimes our lives are like the *doldrums*. It is a hard thing for a sailing man, and they just dream about being with a lady sexually when they pull into port. These are some of the reasons men go to sex."

Red seemed to understand what Papa was saying, but needed clarification, "So, why is it wrong to have sex outside marriage?"

Papa said, "Fair enough, God's ways are not known by everyone. Listen to this Proverb":

32
Whoever commits adultery with a
woman lacks understanding;
He *who* does so destroys his own soul.
33
Wounds and dishonor he will get,
And his reproach will not be wiped away.

34
For jealousy *is* a husband's fury;
Therefore he will not spare in the day of vengeance.
35
He will accept no recompense,
Nor will he be appeased though you give many gifts.
(Proverbs 6:32–35)

Papa asked, "What is this Proverb saying?" Red scratched his head, rubbed his chin, pondered a bit, and replied, "It sounds like God wants to protect us from something." Papa rejoiced and cheerfully announced, "Bravo me, boy, you got it. God's negative commands are given for some positive reasons. He wants to protect us and to provide for us. That is what real love does. What do you think He is protecting here? What does He want to provide you with?"

Red was matter of fact, "Sounds as if He wants to prevent us from destroying ourselves and from hurting others." Papa clapped his approval and said, "Amen, brother. He is protecting you from sickness, shame, and even death. He is also protecting the family unit; you see, sex is for the development of family. God is all about family! I have had all my children memorize the Sermon on the Mount, where Jesus said:

Adultery in the Heart

27
"You have heard that it was said to those of old, *'You shall not commit adultery.'*
28
"But I say to you that whoever looks at a woman to lust for her has already committed adultery with her in his heart.
29
"If your right eye causes you to sin, pluck it out and cast *it* from you; for it is more profitable for you that one of your members perish, than for your whole body to be cast into hell.
30
"And if your right hand causes you to sin, cut it off and cast *it* from you; for it is more profitable for you that one of your members perish, than for your whole body to be cast into hell."
(Matthew 5:27–30)

Red retorted, "You have got to be kidding! Cut off your hand?" Papa agreed and clarified, "That is an over-the-top statement to make a point. Jesus wants us to hate sinning so much that we would rather cut off our own hand than sin. But, He really doesn't want us to cut off our hand. He just wants us to understand how serious sexual sinning is." Red reaffirmed, "I get it." Papa said, "Even some of God's greatest have struggled with sexual sin, and God restored them. Take King David, for example. He committed adultery with Bathsheba. God was disappointed, dealt with his sin, but did a great work in his life. David began to understand his perverted ways, repented of his sins, and became a man after God's own heart." Red said, "So there is hope for a pirate like me?" Papa said, "*Sink me, aye*, there is hope for every man. David went on to pray a great prayer about this. Listen to this passage from Psalm 51":

10
Create in me a clean heart, O God,
And renew a steadfast spirit within me.
11
Do not cast me away from Your presence,
And do not take Your Holy Spirit from me.
12
Restore to me the joy of Your salvation,
And uphold me *by Your* generous Spirit.
13
Then I will teach transgressors Your ways,
And sinners shall be converted to You.
(Psalm 51:10–13)

BASK: Wisdom

Papa took time to explain this story to Reo and then sang to him one of his favorite songs taken from this account.

Breathe on me, Breath of God; Fill me with life anew,
That I may love what Thou dost love,
and do what thou wouldst do.

Breathe on me, Breath of God, until my heart is pure,
Until with Thee I will one will, to do and to endure.

Breathe on me, Breath of God, till I am wholly Thine,
Until this earthly part of me glows with fire divine

Breathe on me, Breath of God, So shall I never die,
But live with Thee the perfect life of Thine eternity.

Breathe on Me, Breath of God, I wear thy CROWN
I know Christ my life, Righteous and Ordered too,
I worship You and walk in nobility.

Red enjoyed this ministry so much that he began to sing along. His Scottish accent made for a beautiful duet. What started out as a difficult conversation about behavior ended with joy because God's grace was abounding.

Gold Nuggets of Wisdom:

- It is about relationships. It is about truly loving God and people.
- Watch over your heart with all diligence, for from it flows the issues of life.
- Know why you have sexual desires and know that God made sex for some beautiful reasons.
- "And now abide faith, hope, love, these three; but the greatest of these is love" (1 Corinthians 13:13).
- True love has the ability to wait. "Love is patient and kind. It is not self-seeking" (1 Corinthians 13: 5). Modesty is godly.
- Be a gentleman.
- Contentment is great gain.
- Anointing: the power to live out of your true identity.
- Fidelity unto God and family.
- Respect God, God's Word, and all God's children.
- Don't just keep your britches buckled up; keep your heart and your motivations pure.
- Remember that God is the "Potter" and you are humble clay.
- Fit in to God's plan; don't try to get Him to adjust to your plan.

Fool's Gold:

- The pleasures of sin come with lasting let-downs.
- Sexual conquest is the way of pirates. (Their booty is shame, guilt, sickness, disappointment, and broken relationships.)
- Pirates are takers only.
- *Splice the main brace.*
- Dice: Live by adrenaline.
- Trice: Hoist your ego.
- Spice: Always add more salt and cayenne pepper.
- Pornography.
- Promiscuity.
- Adultery.
- Infidelity.
- Disrespect.
- Adrenaline, feelings, and unbridled passion.
- Impatience, expedience, pressing the issue.
- Always be about the *chase* and the conquest.
- Raise the *Jolly Roger*; always be on the make and take, take, take. (*Plundering* is the pirate way. If you live this way, get used to the scurvy, the crabs, sexually transmitted diseases, and a numb conscience. Also, realize that as you look back at your life, you will have left many women, children, and families drowning in your wake.)
- Always tell the Potter what to do.
- Never trim your sails; always sail straight away the way you want to. (Many a pirate became shipwrecked because they refused to steer away from trouble and crashed upon the rocks.)

7.

Prudence, Understanding, and Sensibility

After meeting with Papa, all Reo wanted to do was be with Moses in the corral. Moses came to him like an old friend greets you at the café. He let Reo easily put the rope on the bridle. They began to walk, and Moses enjoyed following Reo's simple commands. Christina knew where to find Reo. She stood at the rail, and as soon as Reo noticed her, he motioned for her to come to him. Moses stood still, and Reo lifted Christina onto Moses' bare back. In a very gentle way, Moses began to walk in the circle with Reo clicking his tongue against the roof of his mouth, making popping sounds that let Moses know he was keeping step. Christina loved being on Moses; her joy seemed to know no bounds as her smile sparkled. She had her hand on Moses' long mane and sat upright as if she had ridden all her life. After a good ride, Reo reined in Moses, fed him some sugar, and walked him to the water. Then Reo and Christina sat on the bench outside the corral to talk.

For some strange reason, they both knew that the other had just had a difficult conversation, and they began to get caught up on the happenings. Reo earnestly told Christina he had just talked with Papa and made a commitment to only meet with Christina in the light and out in the open. He said it was good for them to meet at the corral so everyone could observe them. Christina laughed and said, "I didn't know that the people here at Shalom were so serious about how we live." Reo chuckled and said, "Yep, I learned lots of new things about life today, and I think it is all for good. What did you learn, and who talked with you?" Christina said, "That is interesting. Wyndolyn and Esther spoke to me. They were very concerned for me and wanted to make sure I was acting right. I used to rebel and do whatever I wanted, but they made sense to me and seemed to care." Reo nodded his affirmation, saying, "I have never had a conversation like that before; having lived around pirates, people just never cared so much. I respect what Papa said to me, and I think I am starting to understand." Looking out at Moses, Christina said, "It has been a delight to see Moses become responsive to your commands. What we are going through is just like horse sense, isn't it?" Reo said, "Sure is; sure is." They agreed to go to the Bible study in the evening, to sit together, and tomorrow they would meet again at the corral.

Prudence, Understanding, and Sensibility

In the afternoon siesta time, Papa sought out Reo, and they had a discussion. Together they reasoned and reckoned that Reo would still go by the name of Reo. Papa remembered and reasoned that some *swashbuckler* would catch wind about the reward on Red's head and try to capture some bounty by turning him in to authorities. Together they reckoned that it would be good to keep his true identity undercover, but to begin to live out of his true identity in the CROWN. They agreed that reasoning and reckoning was what wisdom was all about. Both men seemed at peace with this decision, and Reo was relieved to be able to live as a free man. Papa pointed out that love covers a multitude of sins and just about everything else, too. These brothers were feeling the love of God and enjoying true fellowship.

At the Bible study, there was energized singing and true enthusiasm about being together in fellowship. Reo and Christina didn't feel singled out in the slightest way because the group cared sincerely about them and had a clear understanding about spiritual growth. When Papa stood to speak, he surprised everyone by talking about the Seven Deadly Sins. He called them the seven "Pirate Attitudes." This was a surprise, because he was known for just explaining the Scriptures—this lesson was a compilation of specific sins and the counter to them. He explained them as Pirate Attitudes, and everyone knew he was talking about the flesh, our innate old ways of living, being under the control of sin, influenced by Satan, and this world's system.

Papa succinctly explained that he believed that greed, lust, gluttony, sloth, pride, envy, and anger were the deadly seven sins he called the Pirate Attitudes. It wasn't difficult for the group to buy in to this understanding, because they were all aware that people go into piracy because they let greed have the best of them. They also had learned that lust and gluttony were common characteristics of the pirate way, and they recalled life in Port Royal—the pirate capital—and it was also known as the "most wicked city in the world."

What appeared to be new to the congregation was his explanation of envy and pride being caused by "fleshly" comparisons. He said that "envy" is comparing yourself to another person, seeing yourself as not measuring up to them, and wanting what they had. And, he waxed on about "pride," being an overrated comparison of oneself to another and puffing yourself up to think you are better than them for any reason. He barely touched on "slothfulness" because he knew they were well aware of laziness and understood this malady full well. He did explain "anger" by telling stories of pirates who felt shortchanged and showed their wrath by wielding their *cutlasses* and drawing first blood. He reminded them that anger is usually the result of believing you are a victim. Papa never allows for victim thinking because he was confident that "in Christ" we are victors. He made sure everyone knew that sin always leads to death and separates people from God and each other. He reminded them that these are called the Seven Deadly Sins for good reason.

Papa stated he wouldn't be a good teacher if he didn't show them God's way, the way of life and freedom in the Spirit. Controlled life they all know as the "current of grace." He emphasized that this is accomplished in a believer's life as they simply allow Jesus Christ to be Himself in them. He said that generosity, purity, moderation, diligence, humility, kindness, and patience are in reality the seven life-giving attitudes of the Spirit-controlled believer who is flowing in the current of God's grace. The congregation seemed to get it. They—in their human spirits—seemed to be saying "Amen!" There was a strong sense of understanding for this teaching, so Papa asked Tim to read Proverbs chapter eight. Tim stood up and walked to the center of the room and read from the pages before him:

The Excellence of Wisdom

1
Does not wisdom cry out,
And understanding lift up her voice?
2
She takes her stand on the top of the high hill,
Beside the way, where the paths meet.
3
She cries out by the gates, at the entry of the city,
At the entrance of the doors:
4
"To you, O men, I call,
And my voice *is* to the sons of men.

5
O you simple ones, understand prudence,
And you fools, be of an understanding heart.
6
Listen, for I will speak of excellent things,
And from the opening of my lips *will come* right things;
7
For my mouth will speak truth;
Wickedness *is* an abomination to my lips.
8
All the words of my mouth *are* with righteousness;
Nothing crooked or perverse *is* in them.
9
They *are* all plain to him who understands,
And right to those who find knowledge.
10
Receive my instruction, and not silver,
And knowledge rather than choice gold;
11
For wisdom *is* better than rubies,
And all the things one may desire
cannot be compared with her.
12
"I, wisdom, dwell with prudence,
And find out knowledge *and* discretion.
13
The fear of the Lord *is* to hate evil;
Pride and arrogance and the evil way
And the perverse mouth I hate.

14
Counsel *is* mine, and sound wisdom;
I *am* understanding, I have strength.
15
By me kings reign,
And rulers decree justice.
16
By me princes rule, and nobles,
All the judges of the earth.
17
I love those who love me,
And those who seek me diligently will find me.
18
Riches and honor *are* with me,
Enduring riches and righteousness.
19
My fruit *is* better than gold, yes, than fine gold,
And my revenue than choice silver.
20
I traverse the way of righteousness,
In the midst of the paths of justice,
21
That I may cause those who love me to inherit wealth,
That I may fill their treasuries.
22
"The Lord possessed me at the beginning of His way,
Before His works of old.
23
I have been established from everlasting,
From the beginning, before there was ever an earth.

24
When *there were* no depths I was brought forth,
When *there were* no fountains abounding with water.

25
Before the mountains were settled,
Before the hills, I was brought forth;

26
While as yet He had not made the earth or the fields,
Or the primal dust of the world.

27
When He prepared the heavens, I *was* there,
When He drew a circle on the face of the deep,

28
When He established the clouds above,
When He strengthened the fountains of the deep,

29
When He assigned to the sea its limit,
So that the waters would not transgress His command,
When He marked out the foundations of the earth,

30
Then I was beside Him *as* a master craftsman;
And I was daily *His* delight,
Rejoicing always before Him,

31
Rejoicing in His inhabited world,
And my delight *was* with the sons of men.

32
"Now therefore, listen to me, *my* children,
For blessed *are those who* keep my ways.

33
Hear instruction and be wise,
And do not disdain *it*.
34
Blessed is the man who listens to me,
Watching daily at my gates,
Waiting at the posts of my doors.
35
For whoever finds me finds life,
And obtains favor from the Lord;
36
But he who sins against me wrongs his own soul;
All those who hate me love death."
(Proverbs 8:1–36)

Papa took plenty of time to explain this chapter one verse at a time. The main thing he wanted everyone to know was that prudence, understanding, and sensibility are important to walking in wisdom. He said, "Common sense is really very uncommon sense." The congregation laughed but fully understood what he meant. Tim did the group a favor by asking Papa to explain what the word "prudent" meant. Papa opined, "To be prudent is to use much thought and consideration in your decision-making. A prudent person will seek counsel and apply scriptural thinking in their decision-making and actions. A prudent person will show, care, and be frugal and conservative in the way they live."

The ladies had made pies and had sweet tea for everyone to enjoy. But before they sliced open the pies and everyone enjoyed the refreshments, Papa took to the center of the group and everyone knew that he had more to say. He said, "I started our teaching this evening by talking about Pirate Attitudes: Remember pirates chased after riches to make themselves great. King Solomon reminds us in this passage that wisdom is of greater value than rubies. You have wisdom; you have something that is extremely valuable. Treasure it, as it brings about true riches and life. Those who sin love death. Jesus came to give us an abundant life. It takes wisdom to unwrap His gifts of wisdom. Let's stand and sing as a choir, "Immortal, Invisible, God Only Wise":

Immortal, invisible, God only wise,
In light inaccessible hid from our eyes,
Most blessed, most glorious, the Ancient of Days,
Almighty, victorious, Thy great name we praise.

Unresting, unhasting, and silent as light,
Nor wanting, nor wasting, Thou rulest in might;
Thy justice like mountains high soaring above
Thy clouds, which are fountains of goodness and love.

To all, life Thou givest, to both great and small,
In all life Thou livest, the true life of all;
We blossom and flourish as leaves on the tree,
And wither and perish—but naught changeth Thee.

Prudence, Understanding, and Sensibility

Great Father of glory, pure Father of light,
Thine angels adore Thee, all veiling their sight;
All praise we would render—O help us to see
'Tis only the splendor of light hideth Thee.
A-men!"

With a holy sense of wonder, the small but vibrant congregation were impressed, not with their singing—though it was reverent and beautiful—but with the awesomeness of God and His wisdom. In a holy hush, they quietly walked to their homes all around Shalom.

The next day Tim, Esther, Nick, Chase, Christina, Wyndolyn, and Reo were assembled at the corral. They gathered to admire Moses and to see how he had developed. The ladies enjoyed being given rides, even though he was still on the rope. After Moses was watered down, the group sat around on the benches and reflected on last night's Bible lesson. Tim said, "That lesson reminded me about how blessed we are to have Papa teach us how to have common sense." Chase laughed at Tim's comment, saying, "You mean 'uncommon common sense!'" Tim retorted, "Yes, that is what I mean." Nick began to mimic Papa and spout off some of his most memorable statements, then the group chimed right in. Before long, they had accumulated a long list of Papa's unique insights into wisdom: They were all appreciated:

- Don't live "high on the hog."
- For breakfast, eat like a king; for lunch, eat like a queen; and for dinner, eat like a pauper.

BASK: Wisdom

- Learn to hold your horses.
- Don't run around like a chicken with its head cut off.
- Make decisions, because sitting on the fence is a sure way to catch splinters.
- Don't pass the buck; take responsibility.
- Rome was not built in a day.
- Don't show the cards in your hand.
- Don't be the person who is not playing cards with a full deck.
- You can't judge a book by its cover. You can't take it with you.
- Don't cut off your nose to spite your face.
- Measure twice; cut once.
- Don't burn the candle on both ends.
- A leopard cannot change its spots.
- Just because a bird flies over your head doesn't mean it has to make a nest in your hair.
- Don't be penny smart but pound-foolish.
- A ship looks good in the harbor, but that is not what a ship is for.
- Don't put all your *cackle fruit* (eggs) in one basket.
- A *Piece of Eight* saved is a *Piece of Eight* earned.
- Don't let a *coin* burn a hole in your britches' pockets.
- Early to bed and early to rise makes one healthy, wealthy, and wise.
- It is not the gale; it is the set of the sail.
- You can lead a horse to water, but you can't make it drink.

Prudence, Understanding, and Sensibility

- A man convinced against their will is of the same opinion still.
- I'd rather wear out than rust out.
- Don't ever let anyone lick the sugar off your candy.
- You can't get blood out of turnips.
- An ounce of prevention is worth a pound of cure.
- The squeaky wheel gets the grease.
- A stitch in time saves nine.
- Strike while the iron is hot.
- A watched pot never boils.
- No matter where you go, there you are.
- Get in the "present"; it is a gift.
- If you don't like the fruits you are growing, then change the seeds you are sowing.
- Sow a thought, reap a habit; sow a habit and reap a lifestyle; sow a lifestyle and reap a legacy.
- It is not how you act, as anyone can be a hypocrite; it is how you react.
- You can't stay on the right path while walking with the wrong people.
- Say what you do and do what you say.
- Loose lips sink ships.
- All that glitters isn't gold.
- God grows beautiful roses on heaps of dung.
- Know that it is love that makes the world go around.
- You can't push a rope.
- Don't be all sizzle and no steak.
- Don't be all thunder and no rain.
- Dreams only work out if you do.
- Actions speak louder than words.

- No mistakes—no wisdom; no experience—no wisdom.
- Bloom where God plants you.
- Your past doesn't determine who you are. Let the glorious future God has for you lift you every day.
- If you don't know where you are going, any ship will take you there.
- There is no free lunch.
- No pain—no gain. Know pain—know gain.
- Get down to brass tacks.
- The squeaky wheel gets the grease.
- It is not about perfect; it is about process.
- God doesn't fit into my plan; I am to fit into His plan.
- Never become dull. Stay sharp.
- Take time to sharpen your ax.
- Discipline yourself so others won't have to.
- Always stay under the spout where the glory flows out!

The assembly had a good time laughing and discussing Papa's words of wisdom. They enjoyed trying to grasp the meaning of each phrase, and together they helped each other gain some new understanding because of these pithy and insightful statements.

Everyone had left the corral except for Reo and Christina; Reo was compelled to tell her his story. He said, "I don't know if you would really want to know me, if you knew my real story. I didn't grow up with this kind of love in my life, and I didn't grow up learning the ways of wisdom." Christina replied, "I grew up in London, and I didn't have much of a family life. I never really knew my father, and my mother couldn't take care of me. I was passed around until I ended up begging on the streets. It was hand-to-mouth in the alleyways and gutters. If it weren't for the taverns tossing their scraps to me, I surely would have died." Reo with real feeling said, "I didn't know you had it so rough." Christina said, "It was demoralizing and dehumanizing. Then the government swept me up and put me on a ship to Port Royal. I was basically conscripted to work in the sex trade. It is nothing I wanted to do. But it did pay and I did get to eat. Some of the girls treated me right, but there were others who hated me."

Reo remarked, "Hated you? How could anyone hate you?" Christina explained, "The sex trade was like begging for food. It is a competition; the first one gets the loot. Some of the girls thought I was taking their business away. That is the life of a prostitute; it is not much of a life." She bowed her head in shame, but Reo lifted her chin with his hand and said, "You have a real life now. God is meeting your needs. You don't have to sell yourself ever again." Christina smiled and then asked, "What is your story?"

Reo said, "I was born in Barbados. I was born to Scottish slaves. England had made my parents slaves. My father was on the wrong side of the civil war when Cromwell was on the throne. When I was very young, my parents had a decent master who provided for us. But because of sickness, my parents and their master died, and I was orphaned while I was really young. I was sold to a brutal master who would beat me and threaten me. I lived in fear. I lived this way for several years until I took a big risk. I swam across Carlisle Bay to gain freedom. I thought I had made it to safety when the sailing men stowed me away in the *bilge* of the ship. But, I quickly discovered that I had made it onto a pirate ship. I was on Captain Hawkins's pirate ship. He was cruel and used fear to run his crew. I witnessed him torturing captives and mistreating women. All I could do to save my own life was to go along to get along. I guess you were a prostitute, and I was a pirate."

Christina said, "That is in the past. We are new creatures now, thanks to grace." They were grateful to God for how He had captured their lives. They hugged and went to their own homes; it was beginning to get dark.

Gold Nuggets of Wisdom:

- Mercy and grace are the way to true repentance.
- Keep an *even keel*.
- Care enough to confront.
- Love disciplines.
- A person with good sense is respected
- Common sense is "uncommon."
- It is prudent to be prudent.
- Walk with the wise and become wise (Proverbs 13:20).
- Pirates do what comes naturally (the flesh).
- Spirit-led people do what comes supernaturally (Galatians 5:22–23).
- It is not enough to get good counsel; we must apply good counsel.
- Know virtue and develop a virtuous life. "Be virtuous." (Prudence, temperance, courage, justice, love, hope, and faith.)
- Wisdom is better than rubies (Proverbs 8:11).
- He who sins against wisdom loves death (Proverbs 8:36).
- Get all the advice and instruction you can, so you will be wise the rest of your life (Proverbs 19:20).
- Make long-term investments.
- Get rich slowly.
- Look for character.
- Practice humility, kindness, abstinence, chastity, patience, generosity, and be diligent.
- Know that good things come to those who wait.

BASK: Wisdom

- Patience is the weapon that reveals deception.
- Keep your deck clear. *Clear the deck.*
- Collect your own wisdom idioms (make this a lifelong discipline).

Fool's Gold:

- Pirates can look like they are rich, but it is not lasting riches. (They are Pyrite-like.)
- Valuing gold more than instruction.
- Being expedient and not principled.
- Chasing all that is shiny. (Like a fish chasing the shiny lure and taking the bait.)
- Believing that you are smart enough.
- Immediate gratification.
- Try to get-rich-quick.
- Only look at people skin deep.
- Be stupid.
- Don't think.
- Always have that *shiver me timbers* dumbstruck look— you know what I mean—have a stupid smirk on your face.
- Always be quick to say, "I didn't know."
- If something goes wrong. always blame. Never take responsibility; act like a victim.
- Practice gluttony, lust, anger, greed, and be a sloth.

8.

Courage to Love and Marry

Shalom is a peaceful place, a place where God's children are learning to work out their relationships through the cross. Papa has regularly mentioned how the cross has a vertical beam—showing how God is always reaching down to us from heaven through the cross—and a horizontal beam showing us how Jesus' death on the cross brings healing to us person-to-person. He explained that this is the wisdom of God—when Jesus became a man to give us the ministry of reconciliation, which he related is the process of restoring fellowship with God and friendships with other people.

Just as Jesus' original band of followers were made up of an eclectic assortment of political extremists, religious zealots, and even unreligious moderates, he had mostly young followers, but some more mature ones, too. His twelve were made up of men, but it was public knowledge that there was a group of women who were very fond of him and followed His every move. Jesus, in His earthly ministry, was all about building relationships. He made it clear that how we loved each other and related with each other would prove His identity to an onlooking world (John 13:34–35).

Shalom is very similar to Jesus' community in the first century. It has ex-pirates, ex-prostitutes, ex-slaves, former conscripts, and an assortment of native Jamaicans in its relational fabric. Wyndolyn comes from a line of Taino and Arawakan Indians who were prospering on the Island when Christopher Columbus came and confused the heck out of the people by saying he represented Jesus; yet, if they didn't find gold for him, he had their hands lopped off. This sent a shock wave of fear throughout the island and created a history of suspicion regarding the Christian faith. Papa came to this island almost 30 years ago as a follower of Saint Francis of Assisi and was committed to a life of ministry service in care for the poor. As a friar, Papa had embraced a life of simplicity, worship with songs, and loving people in Jesus' name. He, too, was totally committed to building relationships in the ministry of reconciliation through the cross. This is why his little community so enjoyed the songs about the cross.

Papa's testimony is all about love; he loves Jesus, and he even left the priesthood to marry Lily because he loved her. Lily had landed in Jamaica because her ship, filled with precious African souls, was in truth a slave ship. It took in water and was unfit to sail and became a reef outside the harbor.

There were hundreds of Africans like her who ended up in Jamaica because of similar circumstances. Their racial differences didn't prevent them from having beautiful and Christ-centered relationships. They discovered the most important and endearing quality in any relationship is to have Christ at the center of it. They knew full well that the most important thing to God is to be united in the Spirit and not to focus on the outward person. Papa loved Lily's heart and she loved his. They ended up not even thinking about their different hues and ethnic backgrounds.

The hallmark of Papa's ministry to this community is the great grace they demonstrate in the ways they work out their relationships with one another. This is Papa's greatest joy, seeing how his children (Esther and Tim) and their community grow in love and enjoy building relationships. In Port Royal, Tim and Esther built a house out of native limestone, and they marveled how these stones were knit together in the wall. It served as a picture to them about their community. Seeing so many different people in their community made a beautiful wall, rocks of different shapes, colors, sizes, and material made for a unique surface the same is true of a beautiful church. The real substance of a church is Spirit-filled people; it is *not* the steeple.

If you were to ask Papa what it is that has made it possible for so many different people from so many different backgrounds to get along with each other and really love each other, he tells you that it is because of the Word of God and the Spirit of God. By singing off the same sheet of music, they have experienced a beautiful harmony. But if it weren't for the Holy Spirit's corrective, counseling ministry in their midst, they would most likely be estranged and wouldn't be the attractive community they have become. The people of Shalom are like the honeysuckle flowers that hummingbirds flutter in. They draw out the nectar of God's love, find a home, and don't want to fly away.

It is Wednesday evening—the night of the midweek Bible study and fellowship. Tonight Papa will be teaching out of Proverbs, chapter 11. As usual, Tim stands to read the Scripture. In fact this community has only a couple of Bibles and both of those are incomplete. Several in the community take the time to write out leaflets of Scriptures on paper made from tree pulp. These precious people love God's Word; it is life and freedom to them.

Tim reads with authority, clarity, and conviction. He doesn't always know how to pronounce each word, but is learning and is helping others develop understanding, too.

10
When it goes well with the righteous, the city rejoices;
And when the wicked perish, there is jubilation.

11
By the blessing of the upright the city is exalted,
But it is overthrown by the mouth of the wicked.
12
He who is devoid of wisdom despises his neighbor,
But a man of understanding holds his peace.
13
A talebearer reveals secrets,
But he who is of a faithful spirit conceals a matter.
14
Where *there is* no counsel, the people fall;
But in the multitude of counselors *there is* safety.
15
He who is surety for a stranger will suffer,
But one who hates being surety is secure.
16
A gracious woman retains honor,
But ruthless *men* retain riches.
17
The merciful man does good for his own soul,
But *he who is* cruel troubles his own flesh.
18
The wicked *man* does deceptive work,
But he who sows righteousness
will have a sure reward.
19
As righteousness *leads* to life,
So he who pursues evil *pursues it* to his own death.

20

Those who are of a perverse heart *are*
an abomination to the LORD,
But *the* blameless in their ways *are* His delight.

21

*Though they jo*in forces, the wicked
will not go unpunished;
But the posterity of the righteous will be delivered.

22

As a ring of gold in a swine's snout,
So is a lovely woman who lacks discretion.

23

The desire of the righteous *is* only good,
But the expectation of the wicked *is* wrath.

24

There is *one* who scatters, yet increases more;
And there is *one* who withholds more than is right,
But it *leads* to poverty.

25

The generous soul will be made rich,
And he who waters will also be watered himself.

26

The people will curse him who withholds grain,
But blessing *will be* on the head of him who sells *it*.

27

He who earnestly seeks good finds favor,
But trouble will come to him who seeks *evil*.

28

He who trusts in his riches will fall,
But the righteous will flourish like foliage.

29
He who troubles his own house will inherit the wind,
And the fool *will be* servant to the wise of heart.
30
The fruit of the righteous *is a* tree of life,
And he who wins souls *is* wise.
31
If the righteous will be recompensed on the earth,
How much more the ungodly and the sinner.
(Proverbs 11:10–31)

Papa thanked Tim for reading the Bible text, and then he drew out its meaning much like we would draw water from a well: We drink what is in it. And Papa only wants us to drink up what the Bible is saying. He says, "This portion is a 'treasure trove' of relationship principles. It gives us some practical insights about how to do our relationships well. As you know by now, we are always about the business of working on our relationships. Ministry is about one thing: It is about relationships, our relationship with God, and our relationships with one another. The valuable thing about relationships with God and people is that they are eternal. It is really sad that pirates don't know this truth, and consequently, they give their lives in the *chase* of things that have no eternal value.

"Once again it is important to know your true identity. You are righteous! You have a right standing with God; you have His character, and you want to do His will.

When we live out of this true identity, the community will rejoice. We rejoice because we will be getting along with each other and relating to one another in love, because love and holiness is God's nature. Please don't forget that love covers a multitude of sins. To do relationships requires that we learn how to love, accept, and forgive each other a lot.

"In this Bible text, Solomon brings us into the blessing by reminding us that as we live upright lives, that means we 'wear the CROWN.' Then we are a blessing to one another, and we enjoy God's blessings together. This is what community is all about.

"This text gives us some practical insights about doing relationships well, such as earning each other's trust, keeping confidences, and being a reliable person. Honor and respect are important matters to consider in relating to people. Once again, we see that this is counter to the way of the pirate. They are all about cutting people down to size, where we are all about lifting up others. So, don't be cruel—rather be gracious because we have received much grace. We need to keep our hearts pure. This helps us keep our motives and intentions right so we don't defraud anyone. Constantly BASK in the sunshine of God's love. Always walk in the light as He is light. Remember to **B**less the Lord at all times. **A**sk Him to meet your needs. **St**ay steadfast in your faith and obedience, and **K**now that He keeps His promises to you. As we bask in His sunshine, He will work out our relationships for us. He is the reconciler.

"He warns us not to be like pigs, like one with a gold ring in its snout. I've seen pirates have rings on their ears, noses, eyebrows. I really don't understand this practice. What is most important is that we let God's good character be real in us and show through in all we do. For example, be generous, like the river that brings the blessing of refreshment wherever it flows. When we live generously, God opens the windows of heaven and pours out His blessings on us. Don't be a reservoir that has no current; let His love always flow like a river. We all know that we can't out give God!

"I will be short and to the point. Don't be like a pirate and trust in riches. We know how that story ends. Try to never bring trouble into your house, be a person who brings 'shalom' (peace). Always be bringing the highest and best good to those around you. If you live this way, God will bless you. He is the source of all blessing, so don't expect your blessing to come from others. If others do bless you, be thankful and show them your appreciation.

"Finally it is important for all of us to be active in sharing our faith with others. Our faith is a contagious faith; it is to rub off on others. Yes, we are to be like a tree—we are like the tree of life. Maybe that is why I like sitting under the mahogany tree and talking with you so much. A tree brings life, fruit, shade, and it will even be sacrificed to build something great. Ask God to make you be like the mahogany tree. Its positive influence is felt everywhere on this island.

"In closing, I want you to know that to do relationships well, we need to know that it is not about us. If you can truly live an 'other-centered' life, you can enjoy doing relationships well; this is where much joy comes from. But, if you think it is all about you, that is the way of the pirate and your level of satisfaction in life will be sunk. Remember Captain Morgan? Well, he sunk the ship called *Satisfaction* to save his own skin. On the other hand, always remember Jesus who regarded others as being more important than Himself and literally gave His life to save us all (Philippians 2:5–11). His reward for living this way is an eternity filled with beautiful and life-giving relationships. This can be your reward, too. My favorite part of Proverbs 11 is verse 25, where it says: 'The generous soul will be made rich, and he who waters will also be watered himself.' I love this—it shows us how God is—it is like the 'Current of Grace.' Those who release grace get grace flowing from heaven back into their lives. Saint Francis understood this well and wrote a song about it. It is called "Make Me a Current." This has been one of our favorite songs. I have asked Esther to sing it, and then let's sing it together."

Esther smiled, turned her gaze toward heaven, and sang as if God was her only audience.

> *Lord make me a channel of your peace*
> *Where there is hatred, let me sow love;*
> *Where there is injury; pardon*
> *Where there is doubt; faith*
> *Where there is darkness; light*

> *Where there is sadness; joy*
> *O Divine Master, grant that I may not so much*
> *seek to be consoled as to console;*
> *To be understood as to understand; to be loved*
> *As to love*
> *For it is in giving that we receive;*
> *It is in pardoning that we are pardoned;*
> *And it is in dying that we are born again to eternal life.*

The community enjoyed mango pies, sweet tea, and sweet fellowship around these important thoughts regarding community. They all took some time to pray for each other and to sing.

The next day Clay, with his bow and arrows in hand, approached Papa to see if Papa would join him at the shooting range for some conversation. Clay wasn't one with a lot of words; he sort of hid behind his bushy red beard and his grizzly bear features. So Papa was quick to walk with him to the range. When they got to the range, Clay set up his target made of straw, stepped off 20 paces, and began to draw his arrows. Under his breath he said, "Steady, aim, fire." Arrow after arrow began to swoosh through the air and were buried in the target, most of them centered in the bull's-eye.

This allowed Papa to break the ice and start the conversation, as he knew that Clay had something on his mind. Papa asked, "Clay, do you know the Bible lesson with this target and the bow and your arrows?" Clay chuckled and said, "What is it, 'kill and eat?'" Papa laughed and said, "Though that is in the Book, the lesson I was thinking about is about 'sin.' The Bible gets its word for sin from archery!" Clay was quizzical and stuttered, "How is that so?" Papa was demonstrative, saying, "When your arrow misses the center bull's-eye, you 'sin' when your arrow misses the mark. Sin means to fall short of God's glory and to miss the mark." Clay let another arrow fly. It split an arrow that was buried in the center of the bull's-eye. With a proud glance back at Papa, he asked, "And what is that called?" Papa said, "That is a good shot." Clay smiled and pumped his fist and let out a roar, "*Arrrr!*" I love hitting the mark. I just don't want to miss the mark with Wyndolyn; you know that we have become good friends. I don't know what to do now, but I want to show her that I am committed to her." Papa said, "Great, friends can become lovers, not a bad idea, huh?" Clay chuckled, stammered, and asked, "How do I go about the next steps in our relationship?"

Papa, taking the bow and the quiver that was filled with arrows from Clay said, "You are ready for the next step because you know that love is a commitment, and you have a good friendship based on Jesus." Clay nodded to the affirmative and said, "I am grateful; she is a good person. I think I love her." Papa said, "You are right, and I see love in your relationship. I think Wyndolyn would be a wonderful wife for you. After all, she is a 'Proverbs 31' woman." Clay with unction shouted, "What, what is a 'Proverbs 31' woman?" Papa laughed and said, "Let's go to the plantation house, and I will open up that Proverb

Courage to Love and Marry

for you. I think you will like it; it will help you with your decision."

At the plantation house, Esther and Wyndolyn are there to greet this duo. They had anticipated their desire for sweet tea and cookies, and Clay gave Wyndolyn a hug. Together with Papa, they expressed their gratitude over and over. After the ladies left for the outdoor kitchen, Papa took Clay into his study and read Proverbs 31, verses 10–31 to him. He read slowly and talked his way through it, explaining some of the meaning.

The Virtuous Wife

10
Who can find a virtuous wife?
For her worth *is* far above rubies.
11
The heart of her husband safely trusts her;
So he will have no lack of gain.
12
She does him good and not evil
All the days of her life.
13
She seeks wool and flax,
And willingly works with her hands.
14
She is like the merchant ships,
She brings her food from afar.

15
She also rises while it is yet night,
And provides food for her household,
And a portion for her maidservants.

16
She considers a field and buys it;
From her profits she plants a vineyard.

17
She girds herself with strength,
And strengthens her arms.

18
She perceives that her merchandise *is* good,
And her lamp does not go out by night.

19
She stretches out her hands to the distaff,
And her hand holds the spindle.

20
She extends her hand to the poor,
Yes, she reaches out her hands to the needy.

21
She is not afraid of snow for her household,
For all her household *is* clothed with scarlet.

22
She makes tapestry for herself;
Her clothing *is* fine linen and purple.

23
Her husband is known in the gates,
When he sits among the elders of the land.

24
She makes linen garments and sells *them*,
And supplies sashes for the merchants.

25
Strength and honor *are* her clothing;
She shall rejoice in time to come.
26
She opens her mouth with wisdom,
And on her tongue *is* the law of kindness.
27
She watches over the ways of her household,
And does not eat the bread of idleness.
28
Her children rise up and call her blessed;
Her husband *also,* and he praises her:
29
"Many daughters have done well,
But you excel them all."
30
Charm *is* deceitful and beauty *is* passing,
But a woman *who* fears the LORD, she shall be praised.
31
Give her of the fruit of her hands,
And let her own works praise her in the gates."
(Proverbs 31:10–31)

Clay was amazed with this text, saying, "I didn't know that the Bible described Wyndolyn this way." Papa laughed and said, "Yes, indeed, Wyndolyn is a virtuous woman. She possesses many godly virtues. This is the kind of woman who would do you good." Clay, shaking his head said, "Yes, but I don't feel that I 'measure up.' I sin, and I 'miss the mark.'" Papa said, "We all fall short.

What is important is that you make a commitment to God and trust Him to help you. It is a sacrificial love that you need, and only God can help you. Jesus gave His life for His bride. He will help you keep your vows if you so choose." Clay said, "I get that."

After a moment of humbling silence, Papa pointed out some characteristics from the "Proverbs 31" woman that he had been observing in Wyndolyn. He said, "I don't think you have any reason to doubt her trustworthiness. You really can't have a relationship with a person you don't trust. She speaks the truth, sometimes painfully, but she does speak the truth. I think you can trust her." Clay responded, "No doubt!" Papa continued, "I think she would only want to do you good; she is a talented woman. She loves to cook and build things. She built Breeze's Café and ran a good shop. She has cooked for everyone here; she has provided for everyone. She has worked way into the night, and we all know that she willingly gets up early to serve the people here. 'Strength and Honor' are her clothing. She has been through so much, I think she laughs at the future, and she lives like she has nothing to fear. I just don't know why she would want to marry you?"

Clay laughed, "I have something to offer." Papa said, "You sure do. I just want you to answer the question, 'Are you better together'?" Clay said, "I think so. I don't want to live without her. She fears the Lord; she is a wise woman. She makes me better—I think she completes me." Papa interjected, "Jesus makes you complete, but she will bless you. She will be a blessing from God. You just need to count the cost. Remember this: Love is a commitment. As soon as you say 'I do,' the feeling might pass away, but your commitment needs to be your anchor."

Gold Nuggets of Wisdom:

- Live truth and earn trust.
- It can't be about you. Water others. Be "other-centered."
- Love is a commitment: It is not a feeling.
- Make friends. Friends can become great lovers.
- Love is for the long haul. For life!
- Relationship with God and people is an eternal thing. Invest wisely.
- Use your head to guard your heart.
- Intentionally build a community of life-giving people. It takes work. Do something every day to build your community.
- Remember in God's kingdom, there are no "little people." Everyone matters to God!
- If you love her, put a ring on her finger, say the vows, and mean it.
- Know the truth: trust-relationship-joy continuum!

Fool's Gold:

- Expecting others to trust you for no good reason.
- Pirates put notches in their belts to mark their sexual conquests.
- Look for a lover (wake up with a pirate).
- Hit and run. Live for the fleeting pleasure of the moment (lasting let-downs).
- Pirates chase things—things that don't last forever. They will all perish in the flames. And sink to *Davy Jones's locker.*
- Let your sexual appetite drive you.
- Only love the "cool" and popular people.
- Live together without the commitment of marriage (without the vows before God). Play house, and build a house of cards.
- Pirates chase at the sight of trouble.
- It's about you.
- Just expect people to trust you.
- Love, grog, rum, and Mary Jane.
- Remember: *"Dead men tell no tales."*
- "In honest work the food is bad, the wages low, and the work is hard. In piracy there is plenty of *loot*; it is fun and easy, and we are free and powerful. The worst that can happen is death or be *gibbeted"* (an old pirate motto).

9.

Be Winsome and Generous

God used Moses to deliver God's children from their bondage in Egypt. Moses, the horse, is being used by God to help Reo discover the freedom he really wants and to take responsibility for his life. For many months now, Reo has been faithful to work with Moses, and he has faithfully taken care of his needs. It has been fun for Reo to give the children rides on his back, and it is especially gratifying to have Christina come to the corral and join him in the training. This has been a safe place for them to build their relationship, and their conversations have been enlightening.

Just as a gardener has to move some dirt to plant his crops, Reo has been dealing with the dirt in his own life. He has found it easy to talk with Papa, Clay, Tim, Earl, Chase, and Nick. To his surprise, he has been able to swap his stories with Christina, and she has shared her stories with him, too. Today he decided to take a big risk and invited these men to meet with him under the mahogany tree, where he begins to dig up some of the dirt in his past.

It is in the heat of the day, and even under the thick branches of this giant tree, Reo is sweating profusely. He is sweating—not because of the heat—but because he has never risked like this before. He knows these brothers love and care for him, but how will they treat him when he tells them that he killed a man? He is under compulsion to confess to the killing of Captain Hawkins.

Taking a scarf from his back pocket, Reo wipes his brow and says, "Brothers, I have invited you here because I believe that you deserve to know the truth about me. My real name is not Reo; I am 'Red,' 'Red-Legs' Greaves." Chase begins to laugh and Red is taken aback, not knowing why he was laughing. He looks perturbed and asks, "What gives, Chase?" Chase said, "I had a hunch; your Scottish accent gives you away." Nick asked, "How does his accent give him away?" Chase reasoned, "He was called 'Red-Legs' because he wore a Scottish plaid kilt. He was known all over these parts." Reo asked, "Why didn't you say anything?" Chase was to the point. "Brother, we all have a past. We believe you are a new creation, and your old life is dead and gone, so why bring it up?"

Be Winsome and Generous

Red struggled, but he picked up on the grace being offered saying, "I am thankful for your acceptance and your forgiveness, but I need to get something off my chest." Papa chuckled, "Go ahead, Scotty, but know that nothing you will say will surprise us or *addle* our commitment to you as a brother." Reo said, "Are you sure?" To a man they said, "Sure," except for Nick who said, "*Aye!*"

Red felt their camaraderie, acknowledged their understanding, and unpacked his story. "While in my early teens, I was sick and tired of being a slave. I wanted freedom, so I seized an opportunity and swam across Carlisle Bay. The ship I swam to wasn't a privateer ship. It, too, was a pirate ship commanded by Captain Hawkins. Some crewmembers helped me by stowing me away in its bowels. My life went from bad to worse. Captain Hawkins was brutal: I saw him torture his captives, and he was notorious for mistreating women. His crew only stayed committed to him because he made them rich. He had a way of landing treasure. I mean, he was making his crew filthy rich; men will do anything to have *loot*. I didn't know what to do, and then he found me out. He almost had me *walking the plank*. I smartened up and went along to get along to save my own skin. But, I couldn't stand for people being tortured, and as we took on prisoners, I stood in the way and protected them. He demanded that I torture them or kill them, and I wouldn't."

Papa laughed and said, "You were between a rock and a hard place." Reo lamented, "I didn't know what to do, and I just knew that I didn't want to hurt anyone. I didn't like being a pirate, but I didn't know any other way of living. I hated Hawkins, and he made a fatal mistake." Nick asked, "What did he do?" Reo shaking his head said, "He had a platter with pistols on it and ship's articles for me to sign. I could either sign the articles and come under his thumb, or take one of the pistols and pace off in a duel. He didn't have any idea that I knew how to handle a pistol." Clay was intrigued and asked, "Did you kill the varmint?"

Reo was fervent, "I walked away, yet in the days to come, he forced me to torture prisoners, and I refused to follow his orders. Feeling threatened, and thinking that he was losing his power with the crew, he again brought out the pistols. It was 10 paces and then fire. I killed him." Chase said, "I heard that you had a fight with him and killed him with your hands." Reo laughed and said, "Pirate stories are like fish stories—they always get bigger with age."

Tim wanted to know the rest of the story and said, "What did you do? How did the crew treat you?" Reo responded, "I didn't know what to do. The crew quickly elected me to be their captain. I drew up new ship's articles, which forbade the harsh treatment of prisoners and women. From then on, we only raided rich ships, but we didn't mistreat prisoners."

Papa asked, "You still commanded a pirate ship?" Reo said, "Yes, I did." Reo, not wanting to justify his behavior, just hung his head. Chase said, "You were in a tough place; we all can relate. I had to sail with pirates, too. That is how I met Tim." Tim smiled, laughed, and said, "God has met with us all in the midst of an ugly world." Reo agreed saying, "My crew really respected me. We overtook a Spanish fleet and turned their guns on the Island of Margarita. We stormed their forts and, to my surprise, we made off with a huge *booty* of gold and pearls. We took the *loot* and got out of there."

Tim, still wanting to know more said, "What is the rest of your story?" Reo, pulling a peace of cowhide out of his pocket, said, "Here is a map where I buried the loot. I want to live in obscurity as a farmer and do what I can to help the poor. I know people on the island of Nevis who can use my help." Clay was miffed and asked, "How did you end up here? I don't know what led you to us?" Reo said, "I wanted out of the pirate life, but because there was a big reward for my capture, they turned me in and placed me in the Port Royal Jail. As God would have it, the day Port Royal was cratered by the earthquake, I was sitting in the Port Royal Jail to be sentenced. I am sure that I was going to be hung for what I had done and for being a pirate. Then the crashing of walls was turbulent; the wall of the jail broke open, and once again I found myself in the middle of the bay. The waters were rough, but I was able to swim out to a whaling ship, and they took me in."

Papa laughed and said, "I can see you must be a good swimmer." Reo laughed and said, "I have that going for me."

As always, Earl had been quiet, but he hemmed, hawed, and stammered, and asked, "How did you end up a free man again?" Reo explained, "This whaling ship was made up of some good men, and they quickly allowed me to help lead their crew. While at sea, pirates attacked us; these stupid pirates had been attacking whaling fleets. I became a pirate hunter and was pardoned for all my previous wrongs. All I want to do now is say thank you to God, simply farm, live in obscurity, and help the poor."

Tim enjoined, "You have had an adventurous life, but why did they call you 'Red-Legs' Greaves?" Red explained, "The Scots are known for their colorful plaid kilts. This became my identity marker. Many of us Scottish sailors were known as 'Red-Legs' as we had sunburned legs." Papa asked Clay if he would sing the thanks song. Clay obliged.

Gracious Spirit, Love Divine! Let Thy light within me shine;
All my guilty fears remove; Fill me with Thy Heavenly love.
Speak Thy pardoning grace to me; Set the
burdened sinner free; Lead me to the Lamb of
God; Wash me in His precious blood.

Life and peace to me impart; Seal salvation on my heart;
Breathe Thyself into my breast, Ernest of immortal rest.
Let me never from Thee stray; Keep me in the narrow way;

Fill my soul with joy divine; Keep me Lord, forever Thine.
Basking in Thy glorious grace; Thy beacon warms my heart;
Alive, free, I am rich in Thee, Lord You are my reward!
My face is set, I bask in Thy glorious grace.

From under the mahogany tree, there was great applause and encouragement for Reo to live the life God has for him. Papa shared a Proverb that inspired everyone to be winsome and generous. He recited Proverbs 19:17: "He who has pity on the poor lends to the Lord, And He will pay back what he has given."

The men enjoyed a good time of swapping stories from the sea and, after all was said, Reo felt loved and accepted. The men were encouraged to know the truth about Reo, and now everyone was free to "walk in the light." They enjoyed true fellowship and vowed to protect Reo. They wanted him to be secure in his true identity. Their lips were sealed.

Gold Nuggets of Wisdom:

- Live in community.
- Be concerned about the care of others.
- Do the right thing.
- Know that God always has a way.
- Believe God to knock down walls: He is good at it.
- Thankfulness opens you up to blessings.
- Ask God to give you His vision for your life. He has one. Look up and meditate on Jeremiah 29:11.
- Always be looking out for the needs of the poor.
- Love and enjoy being in the light. Let truth always be your friend.
- Learn how to swim!
- Develop your leadership gifts. God has given you spiritual gifts.
- Always express your gratitude to God and to your friends and family.
- Love songs about the cross, the blood, and the power of His resurrection.
- Learn to protect your friend's true identity. (*Loose lips sink ships.*)
- Care for the poor. Though Jesus was rich, He made Himself poor to reach the poor (2 Corinthians 8:9).

Be Winsome and Generous

Fool's Gold:

- Just go with the flow.
- Be self-protective and save your own skin.
- To get rich, you must *raid and pillage*.
- Be condescending and bossy.
- Act like an entitled brat.
- *Blaggard* others and blow their cover.
- Treat people like they are *bungholes*.
- Don't trust anyone, and always be on the run. Do the pirate thing and *chase*.
- Stay in the shadows; love darkness.
- Stay in the *bilge* of a stinky and rat-infested ship and worry yourself sick. (Life is like this when you don't walk in the light.)
- Don't care for others; after all you have enough problems.
- Don't give a rip about the poor.

10.

Live, "Fully Alive" (Enthusiasm)

From the beginning of faith, God's children have been "gospelling" the Gospel. God has always had His children pass His faith along by telling stories. From under a tree or sitting around a fire or a table, God's people have had the joy of telling His great stories. Like pirate treasure buried on a secluded island, God has always hidden His glorious Gospel in His wonderful stories.

It doesn't take much enlightenment to see the Gospel in the stories of Joseph, Samson, Moses, Joshua, Ruth, Naomi, and Boaz, or in the exciting story of Esther who saved her people with great courage by touching the tip of the golden scepter. We are a people who wear the CROWN, and we are the people of the scepter, the people of authority and identity as seen in the scepter and the CROWN. Remember, Jesus said, "All authority in heaven and earth has been given to me. Go therefore and preach the gospel" (Matthew 28:18–20). You may ask, "How does the Gospel get preached?" It gets preached when God's children are about "gospelling" the Gospel—when they get excited and actually go about telling His stories. After all, this is what "history" is.

Shalom has been a place rich in this Christian tradition. These precious people love to sit around and tell the stories of God. It doesn't even bother them to hear them over and over again. They reckon that this is how you really learn them, and when you hear one of God's stories, sometimes you see a lesson you overlooked before. Even though you listen to stories, they have a way of opening up your "eyes of faith." God knows this and has made it His way of discipleship and evangelism.

Every Christian has a story, and inside every testimony is the Gospel. Just like in every Christian is Christ; the treasure of every story is the Gospel. Tonight Nick is on the stump; literally he is on the stump expounding about a story that has captivated him for years. This is not a Bible story, but it, too, has the Gospel buried in it like pirate treasure. The story that has lit him up for years has been the story of Captain Henry Morgan and the sinking of the *Satisfaction*. This was the Captain's flagship he sacrificed to save his own skin. Nick is impressed with the irony this story keeps bringing to him and is sure it will inspire those who fill in the circle tonight.

Live, "Fully Alive" (Enthusiasm)

Not far from the outdoor kitchen is a fire circle made up of fallen logs, a fire pit, and a stump for the storyteller to stand on. Jamaica is a land of wood and water, so finding timber for the fire is always easy to do. The only real concern is to keep enough lumber covered and out of the moisture, so it is tinder enough to burn. But everyone loves the fire, and everyone in Shalom loves to see the storyteller stand or sit on the stump and wax eloquently and let a good story start to blaze.

The darkness of the night only makes the glistening fire all the more enchanting. The crackling of hot branches and the lofting flames creates excitement for the story to be unwrapped. Even though the fire is burning hot, Nick is uncorking real energy as he sets up the story by telling about some personal encounters with the famed sea captain. Everyone can see passion on Nick's face, and their spines tingle, as they just know this story lives in the orator himself. Nick's face is aglow with reflective fire, but his heart is ablaze with this crackling story.

He reminded the stoop group where he had encountered the Captain going from pub to pub in old Port Royal. He commented that the rotund Captain was hard to miss because he was so fat. He said that the red-suited *swashbuckler* had to turn sideways to get in some of the tavern doors because he was so obese. He let them know that even though he was going to tell them the story about the sinking of the *Satisfaction*, it was obvious to all that the Captain didn't die satisfied.

He made it clear the Captain—who had become governor of Jamaica—had become a slave to rum and the sugary pastries he regularly devoured.

Nick, who had the pirate moniker of "Neck Beard," was not outwardly beautiful; he enjoyed being scraggily and always said that he had no good reason to shave. In talking about Captain Morgan, he found it interesting that even though the *"Sea Dog"* was rich and powerful, he became poor, helpless, and powerless to his own flesh. The real story, as Nick told it, was the story of how the *"little pirate"* took down the man who was one of the biggest pirates of all time. Nick didn't have the vocabulary to use the word "irony," but everyone knew that on the basis of his sheer enunciation, Nick was amazed with the ironic insights found in the "sinking of the *Satisfaction.*"

Nick had the group in the palm of his hand, and when he told them that he actually sailed with the Captain and was at Lake Maracaibo when it went down, the group was quieted by a dramatic pause. He even expressed his desire to work for the Captain Morgan, at his sugar plantation, and thought that this would surely be a secure job. But he said, "Looking back, I can see that this was no good man to work for."

Assured that he had laid down enough of the backstory, Nick began to set the scene for Captain Morgan's shameful tale. Nick had a flare for colorful language, and as he talked, you could smell the exploding

Live, "Fully Alive" (Enthusiasm)

cannon plugs and feel the wafting blasts of gunpowder that rocked and smoked the air during the battle.

Nick said, "It was a miserable night. The Captain had been terrorizing the coast of Venezuela when the Spanish ships spotted the Captain's fleet of 10 ships. The Captain had been torturing people in these coastal communities and wringing their heads and necks with ropes, squeezing out the information about more treasure and their families' hidden resources. The Captain didn't care—all he wanted was bigger, better, and more treasure. He just wanted to get rich. I thought for sure we had taken too much time in this effort and, sure enough, the Spanish had set a trap for us. Like a hand caught in a cookie jar, we had been grabbing for too much *loot,* and the Spanish had us trapped at the mouth of the lake.

"When we approached the inlet, we could see that the Spanish had their big cannon aimed right at us; we were in their sights and doomed. But, do you think that fazed the Captain, *begad no!* He had only one thing on his mind. He only cared about saving his own fat *booty,* if you know what I mean? In a flash he devised a brilliant scheme. He called his crew to load the *Satisfaction* with gunpowder and to sail this flagship straight away into the Spanish galleon and to hurl the grappling hooks at the ship, so the two would be tied together and equally fatefully bound. Then he had his ground forces head to the sandy beach and march on the land to attack the fort from that point. Just as he envisioned, the Spanish forces then turned their big cannon toward the ground troops; the Captain let the rising tide saunter his ship and his spiced rum out to sea away from firing range. That is all he really cared about. Can't you just see the fat Captain smoking a stogie and downing a pint of rum, while the battle raged?

"A dozen men were sacrificed that fateful night on the *Satisfaction*, and more than 100 crew members died in the ensuing battle, but the Captain and his large rear end were safe and free from harm, protected by the big sea."

The members of the fire circle were engaged in the story, and the popping of the embers only amplified the saga. As these precious souls looked into the flames and heard the timbers popping, it made them think that they could see the ships exploding, and they felt the battle's toil. Then Nick brought them back to the spiritual lesson of this story. He said, "I have learned many lessons from the sinking of the *Satisfaction*. The most important lesson to me is how the little pirate is a *swashbuckler* that will always get us to try to meet our own needs and to save our own skin. Papa has taught us that sin is really attempting to meet our own needs in our own way. This is what Captain Morgan did. And, this is what we do when we go our own pirate-like, sinning ways."

The group was quiet, enthralled, and intent on absorbing this message. It wasn't that more needed to be said; Nick had powerfully related this story to life in such a way that he had them in the palm of his hand. And then he lamented, "I can't believe it, but at the time of being with the Captain out at sea, I felt so big, so powerful, and important. I am ashamed to compare this story to Jesus who laid down His life for His followers. Think about it, He sacrificed His life, and now we are satisfied. Captain Morgan tried to save his own life, and I am sure he never found satisfaction. But those who believe in Jesus are satisfied and never put to shame."

As the fire flickered, everyone in the group was thinking about the significance of the message the storyteller brought. It was a time of introspection. The group knew how to personalize and apply scriptural teaching to their lives, and everyone seemed to be contemplating their own personal response to grace, responsibility, and truth. Then Reo stood up and joined Nick by the stump. He was under compulsion and said, "I think I am the opposite of Captain Morgan. Thanks to God's grace, I have found satisfaction." Nick was encouraged by this passionate response and asked Reo to give an account.

Reo was resolute and began to preach up a storm. He said, "I am so happy to have met you and learned about the grace of God. Through God's Word and by grace and faith, I think I now understand my life story. I never wanted to be a slave, and reared by pirates, who would want that kind of life? I now believe God has saved me for a purpose, and I believe that even though I had a very rough life, God's grace reached me and kept on saving me. More than once, He enabled me to swim to safety. It must have been Him who kept me alive on the boisterous seas and from being killed by pirates.

"My aim was never to be a pirate and capture as much *booty* we could land. Shoot fire, no! I just wanted to live and be free. Now by grace I am alive; I am free, and I know that He is true. I am grateful to Papa Peter and all of you for showing me by the Word of God this way of life. I am grateful that I have witnessed how you live this life. Your example has made me understand how life is to be lived. We have been learning that this is the way of wisdom. God has shown me that true satisfaction is found in Him alone. He is our exceeding great reward. He is our treasure. And, because we know and experience Him in this way, we are now able to enjoy real satisfaction.

"I said I am the opposite of Captain Morgan; he tried to become powerful by amassing a huge fleet. I just wanted to stay alive and experience family. He wanted to be rich. I didn't care if I were poor, and I just wanted to be alive and free. He sacrificed the *Satisfaction* to save his skin. He never got a bit of satisfaction out of this life. Sure he had money, rum, property, and slaves to cater to his wants. But he wasn't alive and free in the Spirit. Therefore he never had true satisfaction. By God's grace, I am satisfied. I love farming, cultivating the ground, planting the seed, and encouraging the growth is satisfying. Making friends with you here at Shalom is satisfying. This is the greatest joy of my life.

Live, "Fully Alive" (Enthusiasm)

By God's grace I didn't have to sink a ship to save my own skin—all I had to do was believe. This is the truth that has made me satisfied. I testify that this is the truth. I give praise to God that by dying to self, I have found life. I don't think Captain Morgan was ever fully alive. Because of your example, I have discovered what it means to be fully alive. This experience has made me enthusiastic about life.

"I believed I was dead in that Port Royal Jail, but now I have found life and satisfaction in Christ. He has saved me. I have become a 'pirate hunter' now that is the opposite of Captain Morgan. He was a pirate provider; he made Port Royal out to be a pirate haven. What I want to do now is make poor people rich. He wanted to make rich people poor. I just want to help people find life, freedom, and satisfaction. To me it is all about being alive, free and truly rich, rich in God! I will need your help to know how to do this."

Nick stepped back up to the stoop. Knowing that the evening story time had found a natural conclusion, he said, "I think God has met with us tonight. Reo, thank you for stepping up and giving glory to God. We are all inspired by our time around the fire together." The group had spontaneously quit feeding more wood into the fire, and it was beginning to smolder. Nick had everyone stand and hold hands and sing a hymn as a prayer of thanks to God. Clay, with his big deep baritone voice, led out and the group sang:

Gracious Spirit. Dwell with me; I myself would gracious be;
And with words that help and heal
Would Thy life in mine reveal;
And with actions bold and meek, Would
for Christ my Saviour speak.

Truthful Spirit, dwell with me; I myself would truthful be;
And with wisdom kind and clear let Thy life in mine appear;
And with actions brotherly, Speak my Lord's sincerity.

Holy Spirit, Dwell with me; I myself would Holy be;
Separate from sin, I would choose
and cherish all things good,
And whatever I can be, give to Him who gave me Thee.

Basking in your grace; your radiance shines on me;
My behaviors flow out of true identity, I am free!
Basking in your glory, I am truly alive, rich, and free!
Spirit of the living God,
Be fresh in me.

The group was inspired by the song, but being under compulsion, the reluctant Clay spoke, "As a blacksmith, I would put metal into the fire, and then with tongs, I would pull it out and place the hot metal on the anvil where I would begin to beat it with a hammer and shape it into the image I wanted it to be. I have come to believe that as a man, we are like metal. We have to be dug up from the earth like iron ore, melted down, honed, refined, shaped, beaten, and polished. And when we go through this process, we can become fully alive and useful to the Master. There is a process God takes us

Live, "Fully Alive" (Enthusiasm)

through. But like metal, we must go through the fire and be placed on the anvil where we let him have us. When we offer our bodies to Him like this, He masterfully shapes us, and then we become fully alive and useful."

The fire was now mere embers, and the group had a whole new appreciation for its warmth. In the afterglow each one reached out to hug their friends and offer some affirming words. The group disbanded with a solemn gratitude to God and quietly dispersed to their homes at Shalom.

When morning broke, everyone was back to his or her work at Shalom. The conversations were all about the fire circle and the powerful testimonies they had heard. Reo was walking around Shalom thanking everyone for his or her encouragement to him. When he met up with Tim, he was curious to ask him about how he could go about serving the poor. He wanted to know how to distribute the wealth he had buried in a pirate's chest filled with gold and pearls. When Reo broached this subject with Tim, Tim counseled, "Not so fast! Reo, I think you need to take some time and get wise counsel. If you just give your gold away, it will be gone, and there will be nothing to show for it in very little time. Jesus said, 'The poor you will always have with you.'"

Reo interrupted, "What then am I to do? I want to be the anti-pirate. I want to help the poor. This is what God has put into my heart. This is why I am on this earth." Tim smiled, and with grace in his voice said, "Reo, that certainly is the work of God. By our flesh we only want to be selfish; to be unpirate-like certainly is proof that God is leading in your life. Yet, I have heard Papa say, 'If you give a man a fish, he will eat for a day, but if you teach him to fish, he will eat for a lifetime.' It will take wisdom to know how to give your wealth away in such a way that your gift will bear fruit that will last. You want to teach people to fish, so to speak."

Reo, looking relieved said, "*Aye,* I get it. You are right. We need to make a plan, a plan based on God's wisdom and His ways. I just want to love life and see good days. I can't think of a better way to express God's love to people than to help the poor. But, you are right; I can't just go and distribute this treasure. I need to use wisdom to figure out how to teach people to fish." Tim had an encouraging look on his face and said, "It is apparent that God has been at work in your life. Pirates certainly don't care about helping the poor. I am happy to see that you know it is not wise to just give it away. Let's figure out how to create a plan and some thoughtful ways that will really help people and create a great return from your treasure."

Being amazed with the wisdom Tim offered, Reo blurted, "How shall we go about acquiring this wisdom?" Tim said, "What do you think about inviting a group to join us under the mahogany tree with the sole purpose of helping us think of ways to 'teach people to fish?'" Reo was delighted. "Great idea, Tim. Tomorrow I will begin to invite group of the more industrious people

Live, "Fully Alive" (Enthusiasm)

here at Shalom to meet with us. Will you help lead that discussion?" Tim smiled and nodded his commitment to help with this wisdom process.

A couple of days later during the afternoon siesta time, one by one a good-sized group gathered for the purpose of helping Red discern ways to go about helping the poor. Everyone who was asked came and was eager to help develop this generosity plan. As Tim had agreed, he opened the discussion by saying; "As you know, God has really done a good work in Reo's life, and he wants to go about helping the poor on some of the islands he has visited. We have talked about one of Papa's concepts of 'give a man a fish and he can eat for a day; teach him to fish and he can eat for a lifetime.' With this wisdom truth in mind, what ideas do you have that would help these poor people and poor communities 'learn how to fish?' He is willing to give his resources, but he wants to release them with wisdom. What ideas do you have to help, Reo, help the poor?"

Wyndolyn was so touched with this approach to generosity that she eagerly shared, "I think we could go to these island communities and help them set up kitchens and teach people how to prepare foods. You know, baked goods and good meals." The group cheered her idea, and Reo said, "That is a great idea." Tim was affirmative and then asked who had another idea. Earl, not one for many words, was rearing to share. He said, "I think you have enjoyed breaking horses. If we take some breeding stock to these people, we can teach them to breed horses, how to break them, and then they would have 'horsepower' for their work." Reo was thrilled with the idea and said, "I never even thought of how horses could create wage-producing businesses and income for these communities." Earl said, "They could learn to build, farm, and transport goods, with horses and wagons."

Tim looked at his good friend and said, "Clay, I suspect that you have an idea or two." Clay said, "Well, if you take Earl's idea of breeding and breaking horses, you would need to have a blacksmith, too. We could teach metal work, and there are many things people can learn to fabricate, like weapons, tools, and ship repairs. This was a real good business for me." Reo was beaming with joy and uttered, "Clay, that is a great idea. Every growing community would need a blacksmith. This could spawn lots of little businesses."

Papa was brimming with positive pride; he was encouraged by the way Reo's treasure could become a blessing to poor people in a variety of ways. Tim, seeing Papa's radiant countenance, called on him to share, saying, "Papa, what insights do you have for Reo regarding this venture?" Papa said, "I look back and see how we had a little vegetable garden in Port Royal. It really opened the door to lots of ministry. And don't forget all the good fruit God gives us out of these luscious trees. That fruit needs to be picked and processed; it, too, is a good business. So, I guess if we teach some of the lessons we have learned from farming, we could help these poor communities develop farming as an industry." Reo was happy for the input and asked, "Do you have a wisdom Proverb that will help us get started right?"

Papa said, "The one that comes to mind is Proverbs 3:5–10":

5
Trust in the LORD with all your heart.
And lean not on your own understanding;
6
In all your ways acknowledge Him,
And He shall direct your paths.
7
Do not be wise in your own eyes;
Fear the LORD and depart from evil.
8
It will be health to your flesh,
And strength to your bones.
9
Honor the LORD with your possessions, And
with the firstfruits of all your increase;
10
So your barns will be filled with plenty,
And your vats will overflow with new wine.
(Proverbs 3:5–10)

BASK: Wisdom

Reo was delighted with the way that Papa could apply the Scriptures to life. He asked, "Papa, could you end our session with a prayer?"

Papa was more than happy to oblige and used the Proverb he had just recited as a prayer. He asked God to give them wisdom as they sought to help the poor. He asked God to help them teach the poor how to fish so they could eat for a lifetime.

Live, "Fully Alive" (Enthusiasm)

Gold Nuggets of Wisdom:

- The truly rich are those who have God as their treasure.
- Satisfaction is contentment in God.
- What does it profit a person to gain the whole world and lose their soul (Mark 8:36)?
- It is better to give than to receive. Live as a river that is a giver. Not as a swamp that is infested with gators. (A swamp is a taker, and so is a gator [Acts 20:35].)
- Helping the poor is like lending to the Lord (Proverbs 14:31; 22:9; 31:20).
- A man is like metal (understand the process of becoming fully alive and useful). Godly women are like precious gemstones. (They have intrinsic value, are beautiful, rare, valuable and desirable, and extremely sought after.)
- Honor the Lord in your giving (Proverbs 3:9–10).
- Be a "good-finder" encourager, and let your friends know that you love them and are committed to them.
- "Gospel" the gospel. Preach the Gospel at all times (Philemon 6).

Fool's Gold:

- Remember the monkey who gets caught because it won't let go of the shiny trinket in the jar. It clenches the object in its fists; it won't let go of the object and is caught.
- Be consumed with saving yourself; you will sink your satisfaction. Don't ever be content. Always chase!
- Loving the world and the things in the world is only the lust of the flesh, the lust of the eyes, and the pride of life. Living this way has no lasting value and keeps people from experiencing life to the full. Loving God is the way to experience the abundant life (1 John 2:15–16; John 10:10).
- Be a reservoir and not a river; be a collector and not a channel, and soon your life will stink. (Vibrant lakes have inlets and outlets. Let the water flow; flow is what keeps you smelling fresh and feeling alive. Rivers that give, live.)
- Just give to make yourself look good. (No, give in secret; God knows your heart!)
- Brag on your accomplishments and show off your prized possessions. (Those who really have it don't ever have to flaunt it!)
- Never allow yourself to be put in the fire or placed on the anvil. Remember: It hurts to be shaped.
- Go *on account* at the drop of a hat.
- Always make *sharkbait* out of those who disrespect you in any way.

- Find the thing that hurts someone and scratch that thing till it bleeds. Be this annoying!
- Live entitled and act as if God, the world, your family, and friends owe you (Romans 13:8).

11.

Loose Lips Sink Ships

Unbeknown to the little congregation at Shalom, Chase had asked Papa Peter for permission to speak to the group at the mid-week Bible study and fellowship time. He had been spiritually aroused by these lessons on wisdom from the book of Proverbs. The group didn't know that he had been spending time in Papa's study digging in and mining wisdom from this treasure trove of wisdom. Tonight Chase was under compulsion to speak to the group; he wasn't known for speaking much. His vocabulary was still chock-full of pirate speak, but with Frieda's help, he will make his points.

Of all things this former pirate could talk about, he is going to give a word on "words," an unlikely subject for a man of few words who spent most of his life saying, *Ahoy, aye, arrrr, begad, booty, C, gangway, shiver me timbers, sail ho,* and *yo-ho-ho!*

As usual, Frieda, his pet parrot, was on his shoulder loving the attention from the group. Chase especially enjoys passing her around to the children, and she always has a word for the little ones. Sometimes she is embarrassing as some of her favorite words are words she learned from pirates in the pubs. Colorful is the word that best describes her: Her bright green coat shimmers in the sun, and the tips of her feathers dazzle with reds, blues, and yellows. She is a classy lady, an uncompromising partner to the rough-hewn sailing man she is living with today. She certainly makes Chase into the most interesting person on the island.

Chase is a much-loved member of this caring community. He has always been helpful, encouraging, and servant-hearted. His key word is "ship-shape," as he knows that *landlubbing* communities need to be in order to stay afloat just as a seafaring ship would. He certainly is a CROWN-wearing man. Like most days, he is topped by his old leather tricorn hat. This hat was a spoil from a conflict at sea, and if it could talk, it would have some wild stories to tell. He wore this hat to keep the sun off his brow and his ears. It is part of who Chase is, and no one in this community calls it a pirate hat because the "little pirate" in Chase has been crucified time and time again.

After some singing, Papa introduced Chase by telling the group that it has been a delight to regularly meet with Chase and study the Word of God together. He said, "Chase is not one for a lot of words. I am sure his words will be few, but he has asked to say a few things tonight. He has also asked for Tim, Esther, Clay, and me to read some Proverbs that he will explain."

Standing tall and with a big smile, Chase positioned himself in the center of the room where Papa stood to teach the Bible. Frieda was right on his shoulder, and Chase tipped his hat back to make sure nothing blocked his eyes. He began to speak, "Ahoy, mates. I have longed to speak with you. Me hearties, I never imagined I would have anything important to say. I was on pirate ships much of my life and didn't learn the king's English on 'em. Thanks to Papa and many of you, I have learned to speak, though I can only read a wee bit. Thanks to Esther and Tim for taking the time to read to me. *Avast*, learn to read, and learn what words mean. And don't be like I was. I was foolish with words. Like a loose cannon, I would let my foolish thoughts turn into words, and I would let them fly. I didn't understand that 'loose lips sink ships.'

"Having been in this study from the Proverbs, I know it is only by God's grace that I am alive today. Tim can tell you I have cast many a pearl before swine. Learn how to detect swine, and then keep your powder dry. When we were on the *Adventurer*, I gave many buckos a piece of my mind that I couldn't afford to lose. I didn't know very many words and didn't know how to express myself. But I tell you straight up that I have time and again said the wrong thing to the wrong person in the wrong way, at the wrong time. I want you to know if you want to live your life to the fullest, you need to guard your tongue. This little piece of flesh that is between your teeth can get you killed, and it can, if used right, bring life to people. Loose lips can sink ships, and if we are not careful, it can sink our fellowship.

"I got so angry and *addled* at *buckos* that I would fire a volley of bad words at them. They threatened to have me *walk the plank*, and looking back, I deserved to *feed the fish* as *shark bait*. One time I made fun of an old *sea dog*. He had a patch on his eye and a hook on his hand. I asked him if he poked his own eye out. He wasn't happy with me; come to find out he did. A pigeon pooped on his head, and he poked his own eye out with his hook. His gang had me keelhauled, and that smartened me up some." One of the ladies asked, "What is 'keelhauled'?" Chase explained, "It is when they put ropes under the boat and make you hang on to them and go into the water, into the dark dank water, and hand over hand holding on to the rope go from one side of the boat to the other. I tell you the boat, the barnacles, and the banging around will beat you up." Frieda spouted, "Barnacles, barnacles." Everyone laughed.

"You could say that I was a slow learner. The little pirate in me caused me to say all kinds of things that about got me killed and could have got us all sunk. I overheard one buccaneer try to persuade the crew to *maroon* me because as he said, 'Dead men tell no tales.' I should have been dead. I tell you the truth; our words can mean life or death. They are powerful, and loose lips sink ships.

"I think the toughest time for me at sea was when we got out of the current, and the wind was bashful. During these *doldrums*, we would get in to saying silly stories. We were full of bilge water and gave ourselves to nonsense and foolish talk. Many a fight broke out when we were in the *doldrums*, all because someone said something stupid. You know, disrespectful, hurtful, or just plain evil. Isn't it interesting that put-downs are so easy for us to come up with and to spew? But, to encourage and edify requires thoughtfulness, prayer, and care!

Beware of unguarded talk. Careless talk costs lives, and loose lips sink ships. Our yappers can get to yapping and, before you know it, you could be *kissing the gunner's daughter,* have your butt over a barrel, and be receiving the 'cat.'" Once again one of the ladies, shouted, "What is the cat?"

Chase apologized, "I am sorry. The cat is the cat-o'-nine- tails. It is nine leather straps with glass, metal, stone, and burrs on the end of the whip, and they rake it over your back to smarten you up. Some don't live through it. It is the same punishment Jesus went through before He went to the cross. Now I can't think of the cat without thinking of what Jesus did for me.

"You know, He died for our sins, and most of my sins were with my mouth. So, don't be a blabbermouth: Learn to buckle your lip. We need to learn to 'right the ship,' and a good word can do that. We need to take heed to our words and know that they come from our hearts. Jesus said, 'From out of the overflow of the heart the mouth speaks.' This kills me, because my words gave me away. My words showed everyone what a bad person I really was. And now that I am in Christ, I have a new way of speaking. Because I don't know how to read well, I have asked Tim to read a verse from Colossians that Papa taught me."

Tim stood right up and read:

5
Walk in wisdom toward those *who are* outside, redeeming the time.
6
Let your speech always *be* with grace, seasoned with salt, that you may know how you ought to answer each one.
(Colossians 4:5–6)

Chase thanked Tim for reading, and then he said, "This Scripture reminds me to be wise with my words. Every time I sit down to eat, I first taste my salmagundi before I put the salt on it. I want it to be seasoned just right. If our words are put downs, critical, or hurtful, we ought to prayerfully come up with something better to say. Or get this, don't say anything at all. Don't be like a pirate—that is not who you are. Let your speech be with grace.

"A new favorite Proverb to me is Proverbs 25:11, which says, 'A word fitly spoken *is like* apples of gold in settings of silver.' One can see how thoughtful a good word must be. We ought to pick our words like you pick apples from a tree, and then sculpt them like a silversmith would make a beautiful locket."

Papa began to clap, and then he said, "What a great word picture. I didn't know you had such beautiful thoughts in your mind."

Chase shook his head, grinned, and said, "You should know that God's Word does good things, it has renewed my mind. Papa, would you please read Proverbs 13:2–3?"

Papa was delighted to lend his support, and enthusiastically he stood and read:

2
A man shall eat well by the fruit of *his* mouth,
But the soul of the unfaithful feeds on violence.
3
He who guards his mouth preserves his life,
But he who opens wide his lips shall have destruction.
(Proverbs 13:2–3)

Chase was happy with Papa's help. He nodded his approval, and then he said, "This is what I have been compelled to talk with you about. The little pirate in us wants us to feast on violence, and this starts with thoughts and words. Guard your mouth and you will guard your life. It is that simple!"

Looking at Esther, Chase asked, "Please read the Proverbs 15 passage." Esther, gracious as always, showed her love for the Word and read:

1
A soft answer turns away wrath,
But a harsh word stirs up anger.
2
The tongue of the wise uses knowledge rightly,
But the mouth of fools pours forth foolishness.
3
The eyes of the LORD *are* in every place,
Keeping watch on the evil and the good.
4
A wholesome tongue *is* a tree of life,
But perverseness in it breaks the spirit.
5
A fool despises his father's instruction,
But he who receives correction is prudent.
6
In the house of the righteous *there is* much treasure,
But in the revenue of the wicked is trouble.
7
The lips of the wise disperse knowledge,
But the heart of the fool *does* not *do* so.
(Proverbs 15:1–8)

While smiling his approval of Esther, Chase said, "This portion shows us the power of words. They can quench violence; they can bring life, and they can be helpful. But, notice how destructive the mouth can be if the little pirate is in control!

"I have learned that it is not how much you know, but it is who you know that matters in life. Because we know Jesus, we don't have to have fancy words. We can use the few words that we know well and help people to understand. I have asked Clay to read Proverbs 17:27–28. He has impressed me with how he has lived this truth."

Clay, with his red face, red beard, and deep voice commanded everyone's attention. He read:

27
He who has knowledge spares his words,
And a man of understanding is of a calm spirit.
28
Even a fool is counted wise when he holds his peace;
When he shuts his lips, *he is considered* perceptive.
(Proverbs 17:27–28)

Chase commented, "True, aye." Everyone responded, "Aye!" Clay was still standing in the place of leadership; a wry smile came over his face as he motioned for Chase, Tim, and Nick to join him for a very unusual song. The fellas had been working on this piece and pulled out some oak rum barrels to beat while they sang this old tune they had reconfigured. It was a song Nick had remembered from a tavern somewhere during his travels.

Boom, ba, boom, boom, ba, boom. The men began to beat on their dried-out rum barrels. Tim used some sticks, and Clay had a hammer, while Chase and Nick simply used their hands to pound out a strong beat from this old barroom brawlers' tune. Clay shouted out, "The Devil doesn't have a tune this true!" And then the men began to sing with deep voices, and pounded out the rhythm on their drums. The men began in unison, and then Clay narrated the story in this foot-stomping song.

Heave ho, Row, Row, Row
What do you know?

Raid, Rob, Pillage
Yo, Ho, Ho, off we go.

Blaggard, Hornswaggle, Complain
Muddle, Befuddle, Scuttle
Land-ho
Loose Lips Sink Ships.
Gossip, Slander, Curse, Cuss
Disparage, Discourage, Disgrunt
Why be so curt?

Cap'n barked:
"Shut ye olde pie hole, matey"

Matey replied:
"But why, sir?"

Loose Lips Sink Ships

The Captain went off like a loose cannon:
"Don't you know, loose lips sink ships?"

The Matey clucked:
"How can a wee word take us down?"

Heave ho, Row, Row, Row
What do you know?

The Captain explained:
"Bucko, don't you know?
Your speech can beach us
Your words can sink us
Words ignite a mutiny
If you don't wise up, you will be marooned.

A critical shout
Brings the "Little Pirate" out.

"Misspeak is a chink that starts a stink
A little fink, and you are thrown in the drink."

Raid, Rob, Pillage
Yo, Ho, Ho, off we go.

Yo, Ho, Ho, and before you know
Shark-bait, Scurvy, and no booty
Feed the fish; want a better dish?
Blaggard, Hornswaggle, Complain
Muddle, Befuddle, Scuttle
Land-ho
Loose Lips Sink Ships.

BASK: Wisdom

Let your words be true
Seasoned with salt
Not too much, serve them just right.

Consider your tenor
Your timing, too.
You don't always need to chime in.
The silent one is taken as wise.

Gossip, Slander, Curse, Cuss
Disparage, Discourage, Disgrunt
Why be so curt?

A word aptly spoken
Like an apple of gold
In a setting of silver.
A beautiful thing, aye!

A carpenter measures
Twice and cuts once.
Don't be a dunce.
Let your words be measured
So they will be treasured.

Heave ho, Row, Row, Row
What do you know?

Ships sink because of
Regrets, Bets, Debts, and Frets,
Think before you light a fuse
When she blows we all go!

It is not how many words you use,
How big, or pretty.

*Just be thoughtful, gracious, and kind
Don't open your mouth and insert your boot!*

*Gossip, Slander, Curse, Cuss
Disparage, Discourage, Disgrunt
Why be so curt?*

*Appeal to the throne of grace
Ask for a word.
He created the world with
The power of Word
You were made new by the Word
Timely words like the tide can lift the ship.*

*Consider your words
Pray over them,
Let God fashion them.*

*Utter them with humility and unction
Speak as if you are speaking for God
Because you are.*

*Let your words be true and pure
Sure to edify.*

*Thoughtful words, wholesome words
Words filled with life.*

*These are the words that lift
And keep the fellows in the ship!
Let your words be:
Respectful, Credible, Noble
Lovely, and Kind*

It is not Yo-Ho-Ho
It is "This I know"

After the song, the group could hardly regain its composure. The crowd was singing along and then gave a loud and raucous standing ovation. After a joyful time of laughter and celebration, Chase motioned for the group to come to order, and then he continued his talk about wisdom in our words. He had Tim read:

4
The words of a man's mouth *are* deep waters;
The wellspring of wisdom *is* a flowing brook.
5
It is not good to show partiality to the wicked,
Or to overthrow the righteous in judgment.
6
A fool's lips enter into contention,
And his mouth calls for blows.
7
A fool's mouth *is* his destruction, And
his lips *are* the snare of his soul.
8
The words of a talebearer *are* like tasty trifles,
And they go down into the inmost body.
(Proverbs 18:4–8)

Chase stood to comment, "These Scriptures have so convicted me, I had to speak to them. Loose lips do sink ships. Loose lips can cause fighting, quarreling, and contention. Remember that James said a loose word could start a forest fire. I can't help but see the *Satisfaction* burning in flames because of pride and loose lips. King Solomon said it clear, 'A fool's mouth is his destruction.' To lie, gossip, and make up hurtful stories about someone seems harmless, but it is like eating rat-infested food and drinking from a poisoned cask in the bilge. Tim, would you read the next ones?"

Tim was bashful and said, "I have not thought this deeply about words before. You have my attention. And he read with humility:

12
Before destruction the heart of a man is haughty,
And before honor *is* humility.
13
He who answers a matter before he hears *it*,
It *is* folly and shame to him.
(Proverbs 18:12–13).

A brother offended *is harder to win* than a strong city, And contentions *are* like the bars of a castle. A man's stomach shall be satisfied from the fruit of his mouth; *From* the produce of his lips he shall be filled. Death and life *are* in the power of the tongue, And those who love it will eat its fruit (Proverbs 18:19–21).

Chase commented, "Loose lips can so offend a friend, that he won't be your friend anymore. This is the tragedy

BASK: Wisdom

of loose lips. Yet thoughtful words are very satisfying. It takes meditation and prayer to know what to say. It is important to learn this lesson because death and life are in the tongue."

Papa was next to Chase holding the open Bible, and Chase asked him to read the passage on his lap. Papa smiled and stood to recite:

18
Pride *goes* before destruction,
And a haughty spirit before a fall.
19
Better *to be* of a humble spirit with the lowly,
Than to divide the spoil with the proud.
20
He who heeds the word wisely will find good,
And whoever trusts in the LORD, happy *is* he.
21
The wise in heart will be called prudent,
And sweetness of the lips increases learning.
22
Understanding *is* a wellspring of life to him who has it.
But the correction of fools *is* folly.
23
The heart of the wise teaches his mouth,
And adds learning to his lips.
24
Pleasant words *are like* a honeycomb, Sweetness to the soul and health to the bones.
(Proverbs 16:18–24)

Chase lamented, "I wish I had known this before I ever set foot on a ship. Our pride comes out in our words, and there are consequences to what and how we say things. Be wise, be prudent, and be pleasant, then your words will be helpful and healthful. Pleasant and gracious words are more difficult to come up with than curse words. Pirates can fire off a volley of curses faster than you can say *shiver me timbers*. Sadly they don't know many words; all they know is pirate speak. It wasn't until I joined this fellowship and learned the Word of God that I learned some good words to speak. Pirates are rude, crude, and tattooed. They talk like pirates because behavior currents out of identity. That is who they are. But, that is not who we are. We have been blessed; we have been saved by grace. So, blessings and grace flow from our saved hearts and off our lips. *Avast, mateys*, learn words that bless and release grace. Bless and curse not. Pleasant words are like honey, they satisfy. They are sweetness to the soul.

"It is true that loose lips sink ships; I've seen mutiny because a man *blaggarded* a comrade with words. It could happen here, if we allow for sedition among our ranks; our sweet fellowship could sour. I've learned hard lessons, and this is a hard lesson. Our words either build up or tear down. Take your thoughts and your words seriously. Don't be a fool.

"Papa, would you read the last Scriptures I have selected and make the final comments?"

Papa said, "Chase, thank you for this exhortation. This is a strong and much needed reminder to all of us." Then, opening the pages he read:

23
Do not speak in the hearing of a fool, For he will despise the wisdom of your words.
(Proverbs 23:9)

1
Do not boast about tomorrow,
For you do not know what a day may bring forth.

2
Let another man praise you, and not your own mouth;
A stranger, and not your own lips.
(Proverbs 27:1–2)

11
A fool vents all his feelings,
But a *wise man* holds them back.
(Proverbs 29:11)

Papa remained quiet for a while, and then he said, "This has been a powerful wisdom lesson. Thank you, Chase." The congregation whispered their approval, and a few "Amens" rang out. Papa concluded. "He who guards his mouth, guards his life." God's Word is so helpful to us. Guarding our lips requires wisdom, wisdom that is now available to us by His Word and by His Spirit. Loose lips do sink ships, but thoughtful, truthful words of blessing filled with grace will keep our fellowship afloat. Let's pray!"

Gold Nuggets of Wisdom:

- You can't go wrong speaking the Word of God in the Spirit of God.
- God inhabits His praises.
- Be careful what you say to a fool. Don't be foolish!
- Pride goes before destruction; if you are puffed up, it is best to shut up.
- Guard your mouth—this practice will preserve your life. Filter your words by the Word of God. (Look at Philippians 4:6–8.)
- Season your words with grace as you would season your food. Taste and see what it needs; people always need grace. You would never season your salmagundi without tasting it first.
- If you can't think of kind, nice, and uplifting words, then don't say anything at all. When you keep your mouth buttoned up, people will think you are wise.
- Learn good words. Expand your vocabulary by becoming a good reader. Don't just add big words to impress people, but add the words that will give your listeners understanding and encouragement.
- Listen to your words and even the tone; it will illuminate what is going on in your own soul.
- If you are angry, temper your words. Words are like feathers in a pillow. If you break it open, you can never catch them and put them back in the sack.

Fool's Gold:

- Be loud and obnoxious; always seek to draw attention to yourself.
- "If you speak with the tongues of men and angels, but do not have love in your heart, you are just a noisy gong or a clanging cymbal" (1 Corinthians 13:1).
- Many words. (Some people think the more words, the better. Truth: Where there are many words, sin is not absent.)
- Smile and lie. (The little pirate in us is capable of smiling and telling whoppers. It is possible that if you tell the lie long enough, you will start to believe it yourself.)
- Be condescending: Look down on other people and act as if they are beneath you. Act like a big shot and use big powerful words to impress yourself and others. But, remember this: God is not impressed.
- Brag and embellish your accomplishments.
- Exaggerate what you know, what you have done, what you have, and whom you know. (Before long you will be the only friend you have to yourself. You will start talking to yourself, and people will think you are insane. You won't even like yourself.)
- Use pirate speak and curse like a sailor. (Pirates try to make themselves feel better about themselves by talking big. Pirates are rude, crude, and tattooed!)

- Always win the argument and never say I am sorry or I was wrong. (This is the pirate way; be more concerned about winning the soul than the argument.)
- Believe that your words don't matter. Never take responsibility for what you have said. Loose lips can't really sink a ship. (Or can they?)
- Have poisoned (curse) words on the tip of your tongue; fake as if you are listening and then harpoon your victim as soon as you can launch in. (If you do this, you will never get a promotion, earn respect, or gain God's perspective. Always try to sift the kernel of truth out of every difficult conversation you have.)

12.

BASK in the Story

"Nice legs, Reo!" yelled Tim as he was smitten by the sight of Reo standing proud on his bamboo raft in the middle of the Rio (river) Cobre, basking in the glory of God and the warm sunshine. What impressed Tim the most was the tartan plaid kilt Reo was wearing. It was beautifully knit with deep blues, yellow, green, and red threads. Held up around his waist by a corded belt, his white linen blouse was blowing in the breeze. This stunning picture put a lump of gratitude in Tim's throat. He couldn't have been more delighted to see his friend own his true identity and embrace a life of freedom in the current of God's grace. Reo was truly alive and free, basking in the acceptance he had found in true Christian fellowship and God's forgiveness.

Regularly the spiritual leaders of Shalom would call for a day of Jubilee, and this church family would gather down by the river to picnic, fellowship, worship, and play all kinds of games, including the raft races on the Rio Cobre. A few years ago when Tim and Esther honeymooned, they traveled to the Blue Bay. Along the way, they enjoyed rafting down the Rio Grande, and they used bamboo rafts tied together with hemp cord. Nick met them along the way and helped them assemble their first raft. Tim called this raft the *Adventurer* to commemorate God's faithfulness to him—to safely bring him to Port Royal on a pirate ship of the same name. He now knew for sure that this abundant life God has given him with Esther is a great adventure. Being on the river and riding on top of the water was a great joy for Tim and reminded him of Jesus walking on the water. Every time he rode his raft on the water, he would look toward heaven and laugh and bask in the sunshine of God's love. The Bible says that the righteous have radiant faces. Tim's face glowed like Moses' face when he came down from the mountain with the precious tablets.

For this special day, Nick helped Reo put together his bamboo raft. He named his raft the *Whaler* to remember the whaling ship that saved his life and later turned it into a pirate-hunting ship. Papa Peter's raft is called the *Satisfaction* to spoof the ship that Captain Henry Morgan sank. Everyone knows that, to Papa, there is nothing more satisfying than being with his family of faith, on the banks of the Rio Cobre, celebrating the life, love, and freedom they have in Jesus.

The first river riders in the first race of the day are Papa on the *Satisfaction*, Reo on the *Whaler*, and Tim on the *Adventurer*. The riders captain their rafts by standing on the raft, and with a long pole, they guide and ride their rafts down the river, standing on the water and poling. There is real spiritual application here. Today's race is only about a half a mile, and Earl will meet them at the finish line and haul them back up the river with his horse-drawn wagon for the next race. This is a fun day for everyone. As the race gets under way, Tim took a commanding lead with the *Adventurer*, and then Papa on the *Satisfaction* took dead aim at the *Whaler*. Reo beached the raft and was marooned on a sand bar. But before you could shout *"shiver me timbers,"* Reo was running in the shallows with his kilt dancing on top of the water; then he dove into the deep and swam under the *Satisfaction*, and the raft began to list. Papa, trying with all his might to keep standing, was shuffling his feet, bouncing on the water, and the raft was tilting back and forth with Reo hoisting the *Satisfaction* from under the water. Reo was just toying with Papa; then he yanked on one side of the raft, and Papa was hurled into the river, making a big splash. Everyone on the riverbank was enjoying the show.

These were grown men playing like schoolchildren in a tub of water. Splashing and trying to submerge each other in the river, soon they both became exhausted. This was a fun and joyful expression of their love for each other. The crowd on the beach applauded their delight. They were cheering, laughing, and shouting their encouragement to Reo and to Papa. The crowd enjoyed the water fight they were able to witness. Tim heard the commotion and saw the unmanned rafts floating his way, and he saved them. With Earls' help, they captured the rafts and placed them on the wagon, and then they picked up Papa and Reo, who were now walking arm-in-arm in Christian love. They were kicking up water as they made their way to Tim and Earl with the horse-drawn wagon. Earl just shook his head and laughed. Tim said, "That wasn't much of a race." Papa said, "There is more to life than winning."

When they arrived at the picnicking party, Reo and Papa were making fun of each other with clever and condescending remarks. Papa said, "It is a good thing you know how to swim; that skill saved your life again." Reo remarked, "I have become a pirate hunter. Whatever it takes to hunt down pirates, I was able to take down the *Satisfaction* without firing a single shot." Papa retorted, "And I was able to beach the *Whaler* with ease." Reo laughed and said, "Let's race again. That was a blast!" Tim chimed in saying, "You two weren't much competition."

The group enjoyed the good-natured chiding that was going on. But quickly the group began to cheer for the new group of river riders who had positioned themselves at the starting line and were standing on their rafts ready to ride the river. Clay, Nick, and Chase were quite a sight on their rafts. Chase had Frieda the parrot on his shoulder, and she seemed to enjoy the action, squawking up a joyful storm. This race was rather uneventful with Clay winning just because he was so strong and able to push it with power.

While on the bank, Papa told the group, "I love these raft races because they are so freeing. It is fun standing on the water and being carried along. It reminds me of the Spirit-directed life. I like to think of the Christian life in this way. As you know, the current of grace flows from the throne of God and leads us all the way to heaven. Jesus said, 'From within you will flow a river, a river of life.' We know that this is the Spirit-led life that He promised. For this reason I believe we should always be optimistic, hopeful, and enthusiastic."

Everyone was encouraged by Papa's words, but some in the group had a quizzical look on their faces. Esther asked Papa, "Would you explain those 'big words' to us, please?" Papa said, "These are really good words: 'Optimism' is the outlook or predisposition to look at life from a favorable point of view. We should always be thinking and leaning this way because of God's grace. Grace means 'favor,' and in other words, it means that God is for us. We are people who have hope—as we have studied before, we know that hope is a confident expectation about the future. We have studied God's Word; we know how things end. We win. Jesus comes for us, and the future for believers in Jesus is bright. Enthusiasm is one of my favorite words; it means to be filled with God. That is what a Christian person is. Jesus came for us so He could establish His kingdom in us.

We are people who are possessed by God; therefore we can be enthusiastic because we have God dwelling in us. We are filled with God. God is with us; He is in us, and He is for us. This is the basis for our enthusiastic attitudes and our hope.

"All around Jamaica we see these beautiful trees. We love the mahogany trees, the castor bean trees, the mango, the avocado tree, and all the fruit trees. They all produce seed and have life in them. We are the same way. We have been born again by God's Word, which is seed. His word is imperishable, and that means we are imperishable, too. We will live forever with Jesus. This is why we are naturally optimistic, hopeful, and enthusiastic as a people.

"We have enjoyed life at Shalom; it has been fun to learn how to farm. Let's review how farming has shown us the 'way of wisdom' with respect to our attitude about life. We are learning to cultivate joy, and this is how we do it. We make sure the Word of God is regularly planted in our souls. We then fertilize the good soil of our hearts with faith. The battle is always the 'battle of believing.' We intentionally 'weed out' the negative attitudes and the unbelieving thoughts from our minds and from our speech. We make sure we bask in the sunshine of God's love—we become like the river with the constant flow of water, this is a beautiful picture of the river of life Jesus talked so much about. The water is an illustration of the Spirit of God in our lives—if we stay in this life-giving river of grace, and flow in the current—we are sure to grow for the glory of God.

Sure, we must regularly prune out the dead wood of bad thoughts and bad habits. But, this is the normal Christian life, and a glorious life it is. Spiritual growth doesn't happen by accident. You must make sure you are planted in the good soil—that means you must intentionally place yourself in fellowship with life-giving people. Do not leave your 'peer-group' to chance. Make sure you are always building up your friends in this holy faith, because there will be days when you need them to build you up. Our faith is an active and enthusiastic faith!

"I brought some of my favorite Proverbs that speak to this winsome attitude that God wants for all of us. Here is a favorite of mine from Proverbs 15:13–15":

13
A merry heart makes a cheerful countenance,
But by sorrow of the heart the spirit is broken.
14
The heart of him who has
understanding seeks knowledge,
But the mouth of fools feeds on foolishness.
15
All the days of the afflicted *are* evil,
But he who is of a merry heart *has* a continual feast.
(Proverbs 15:13–15)

"You just have to love the word 'merry.' It means to be cheerful and joyful. This is a delightful word. It's just like us splashing out in the river; we are happy and alive because of God's love for us. It is a choice, and yes, you can choose to be unhappy, bleak, blue, dejected, gloomy, and down in the mouth, but these attitudes are not consistent with our true identity. It is not who we really are. We are CROWN–wearing children of the king who are fully alive and engaged in the abundant life. Remember the CROWN stands for Christ who is our life and righteousness because we are accepted in the Beloved and have His holy nature in us. Order is becoming to us because God is a God of order. Therefore we order our lives according to His Word and His ways. We worship our way through life. We sing and even work as unto the Lord. This is our spiritual service. And lastly we walk in nobility. We know that behavior always flows out of identity. Our study in the Proverbs has confirmed this truth. You know who you are; you..." Then the group in unison shouted, "Wear the CROWN."

Papa laughed with joy and said, "You get it, and you are my joy! I brought a few more Scriptures on this topic. Listen to these texts:

22
A merry heart does good, *like* medicine,
But a broken spirit dries the bones.
(Proverbs 17:22)

"I believe this is for real: If we cultivate a merry heart, even our physical bodies will be healthier, and we will feel better. We all want to feel good, so I say practice tuning your heart to be merry. If you do this, you will enjoy life more and have more friends. You will help others apply faith to their lives, too. A 'believer' really ought to live like he or she believes! Faith really does make all the difference.

"There are many benefits that go along with these wisdom principles. What I really want to pass along to each of you is the personal discipline and routine of daily meditating on a Proverb. There are 31 of them, and just about that many days in each month. What do you say—let's make it our daily practice, or routine. You know that the 'rut of routine can be the groove of grace.' Don't forget the benefits of Scripture memory. Regularly hide God's Word in your heart, and then the Holy Spirit can easily bring to your remembrance a promise, a command, or a word of encouragement just when you need it. This discipline has been a great help to me." Then from his memory Papa began to recite:

2
To know wisdom and instruction,
To perceive the words of understanding,
3
To receive the instruction of wisdom,
Justice, judgment, and equity;

4
To give prudence to the simple,
To the young man knowledge and discretion—
5
A wise *man* will hear and increase learning,
And a man of understanding will attain wise counsel,
6
To understand a proverb and an enigma,
The words of the wise and their riddles.
7
The fear of the L<small>ORD</small> *is* the beginning of knowledge,
But fools despise wisdom and instruction.
(Proverbs 1:2–7)

"I know that I got a little carried away with this teaching today. Let's quote together Colossians 3:1–4. I just want to remind you who you are."

Papa started saying the first few words, and then the group was able to complete the text because they were so familiar with it:

1
If then you were raised with Christ, seek
those things which are above, where Christ
is, sitting at the right hand of God.
2
Set your mind on things above, not
on things on the earth.

3
For you died, and your life is
hidden with Christ in God.
4
When Christ *who is* our life appears, then you also
will appear with Him in glory.
(Colossians 3:1–4)

Esther stood up, looking radiant and caressing the baby bundle in her belly, and said, "Let's sing, *I BASK in Your Grace*":

I have done wrong
Sin pains my heart
I need the sunshine of Your love

Rinse away the damming guilt
Wash away the silt
Vanish the grimy cloud

Your Word tells me
I am clean
Faith helps me to see
I bless You, God

My feelings confuse my soul,
Adjust my mind to truth
The reality of the blood

Help me to choose
To obey, stay and
Walk with You.

BASK: Wisdom

I stand by grace
So I ask

Like a stupid sheep
Yet I go astray,
I know all have sinned
Help me to quit dead-end thoughts

I have done wrong
Sin pains my heart
I need the sunshine of Your love

I have sinned against you
Evil tries to ruin me
I stay abiding in You

I deserved Your judgments
Against me

Rinse away the residue
Of pride and self-will
I want to do Your will
Make me loyal and real
Let me practice your presence

I love to be alive and free
My true reward is You
I am rich in God
Basking in:
The sunshine of Your love.

Comforted by Your presence
Pleasant warmth, glorious joy

I live in the sunshine
Of Your love

I have been saved
My heart is made new

Lifting hands to say:
I bask in Your grace
I see the smile on your face.
By your Spirit
I know I am Yours
Alive and free
Singing ABBA,
I love You!

Basking in the sunshine of your love
Buoyant in the current of your Spirit
I am alive, free and rich,
I bask in your grace.

This precious community of believers enjoyed the rest of the day at the river. The races were fun; the food was delicious, and the conversations under the shade trees were God-honoring and encouraging. This day was a blessing to everyone because the spiritual leaders made the decision to dedicate this day as a day of Jubilee for this purpose.

Papa was compelled to say one more thing. He said, "Never forget the importance of making good decisions. This is one of the benefits of the book of Proverbs. It will encourage you to make decisions and impart to you the values that go into making good decisions. You will discover that the quality of your life will depend largely on the quality of your decisions. This book of Proverbs really is a treasure for you to uncover every day. Remember King Solomon was considered the wisest man who ever lived, and he was very rich, too. I am just giving you the 'lay of the land.'"

The men had assembled a fire pit, and the men who had been fishing returned, cleaned their fish, and were frying them on the fire in coconut oil. Everyone was anxious to partake of the feast. As usual there were lots of fruit-filled pies for everyone to enjoy. Everyone pitched in a little so the group could rest, relax, and enjoy this day of Jubilee. This day was a marvelous way to experience God's grace.

Papa slipped away with a piece of mango pie, and from under a castor tree, he reflectively gazed at the group and was amazed with how far they had come and what God had brought them through. With gratitude in his heart, he prayed as he gazed. With a lump in his throat he prayed over Tim and Esther who were pregnant again, Tim holding Esther on his chest with his hand on their baby in Esther's belly. There was Clay and Wyndolyn enjoying each other and playing cards with Nick and Chase. Christina was riding Moses the horse as Reo was walking them along the river side. Earl was giving the children rides behind Onyx, one of his prized Belgian steeds.

Reo would later follow his heart and the scratches he etched on the leather hide of his treasure map. He found the spot and dug up his buried treasure, and like a good farmer, he planted these riches with wisdom into lives of poor people. God's Word was like seed, and it flourished and helped him grow. Red would be known as a kind man who gave his life to helping the poor. He lived a respectable life on the island of Nevis as a gentleman farmer and gave generously to his community.

BASK: Wisdom

Gold Nuggets of Wisdom:

- Let grace flow into your life by having "Days of Jubilee." (Set aside days to rest and relax. Have fun!)
- Choose to be optimistic. It looks good on you, and it will give you a good disposition.
- Be hopeful. You are promised a glorious future.
- Enthusiasm is consistent with your true identity. God is in you. Remember the power of seed. (If you don't feel enthusiastic, meditate on the Word and let this imperishable seed well up within you.)
- Always be working on your life-support network. Your friends will be there for you if you are there for them.
- Choose to be cheerful; it will even make you healthy!
- Build fun into your life.
- Let the "joy of the Lord be your strength" (Nehemiah 8:10).
- Live out of your anointing (1 John 2:20, the ability to appropriate your true identity: Jesus!).
- Know the laws of sowing and reaping (Galatians 6:7–10).
- If you want good friends, be a good friend.
- Read and meditate on a Wisdom Proverb every day. (Maybe this is why there are 31 of them?)
- Establish good routines, and they can become a groove for grace.

- Let your speech always be with grace. Show respect for God and people in the way you choose and utter your words.
- Discipline yourself so others won't have to.
- You know who you are. You wear the CROWN!
- Always think about heaven. This is your true home and your glorious future (Colossians 3:1).
- Be a river! Flow in the current of God's grace.
- Always ask: "What would Jesus do?"

Fool's Gold:

- Work all the time and don't ever rest.
- Be a reservoir and not a river (Don't flow; just accumulate stuff so that you will be stagnant and stink.)
- Don't have discipline or good routines. Just do whatever you want to do. (Then you will have to be disciplined harshly by the authorities, maybe even *gibbetted.)*
- Choose to be depressed and you will be.
- Live by adrenaline. Be driven and obsessed with personal success.
- Choose to be negative and you will talk yourself into being sick.
- Speak like a pirate. *Aaargh!* Use negative words and repel people.
- Think as if the world is all about you, and that the world revolves around you. (Then you will make everyone around you sick, too.)

Songs and Authors
WISDOM

Chapter One:
   "All Creatures of Our God and King"
      By Saint Francis of Assisi
   "Bringing in The Sheaves"
      By Knowles Shaw

Chapter Two:
   "All People that on Earth do Dwell"
      By William Kethe

Chapter Three:
   "Praise My Soul the King of Heaven"
      By Henry Francis Lyle

Chapter Four:
   "Beautiful Hummingbird"
      By Sid Huston 2017

Chapter Five:
   "Channels Only"
      By Mary E. Maxwell

Chapter Six:
   "Breathe on Me, Breath of God"
      By Edwin Hatch 1886, Robert Jackson 1894
         4th verse by Sid Huston

Chapter Seven:
"Immortal invisible, God Only Wise"
By Walter Chalmers Smith

Chapter Eight:
"Lord, Make me a Channel"
By Saint Francis of Assisi

Chapter Nine:
"Gracious Spirit, Love Divine"
By John Stocker,
5th verse by Sid Huston 2017

Chapter Ten:
"Gracious Spirit, Dwell With Me"
By Thomas T. Lynch 1855, Richard Redhead 1853
4th verse by Sid Huston 2017

Chapter Eleven:
"Loose Lips Sink Ships"
By Sid Huston 2017

Chapter Twelve:
"I Bask In Your Grace"
By Sid Huston 2017

Scripture Index
WISDOM

Bible references include:

Chapter One: Bringing In the Sheaves
　　Proverbs 13:20
　　Romans 5:3-6
　　James 1:1-3
　　Romans 13:8

Chapter Two: Beware of Pirates
　　Proverbs 1:10-19
　　Proverbs 6:16-19
　　Proverbs 8:36
　　Ephesians 1:6
　　1 Corinthians 15:33
　　Colossians 2:6-10

Chapter Three: The "Real"' Pearl Story
　　Matthew 13:45-46
　　Proverbs 3:1-35
　　Colossians 3:1-4
　　Revelation 12:10
　　1 Samuel 16:7
　　James 1:1-3

Romans 5:3-6

Chapter Four: The Hummingbird
    Proverbs 4:1-27
    Proverbs 13:20
    2 Timothy 2:15
    Hebrews 11:1,6

Chapter Five: Earl's "Broken" Horses
    Proverbs 21:2-4
    Proverbs 11:2-4
    Matthew 5:3-5
    Isaiah 66:1-2
    Proverbs 22:4

Chapter Six: Pirates Are Liars, Perverted and Bound
    Proverbs 5:1-23
    Proverbs 6:20-29,32-35
    Matthew 5:27-30
    Proverbs 5:10-13
    Psalm 51:10-13
    1 Corinthians 13:5,13

Chapter Seven: Prudence, Understanding, and Sensibility
    Proverbs 8:1-36
    Proverbs 13:20
    Galatians 5:22-23

Chapter Eight: Courage to Love and Marry
    Proverbs 11:10-31
    Proverbs 31:10-31

John 13:34–35
Philippians 2:5–11

Chapter Nine: Be Winsome and Generous
　Proverbs 19:17
　Jeremiah 29:11
　2 Corinthians 8:9

Chapter Ten: Live, "Fully Alive" (Enthusiasm)
　Proverbs 3:5–10
　Matthew 28:18–20
　Mark 8:36
　Acts 20:35
　Proverbs 14:31; 22:9; 31:20
　Philemon 6
　1 John 2:15–16
　John 10:10
　Romans 13:8

Chapter Eleven: Loose Lips Sink Ships
　Colossians 4:5–6
　Proverbs 25:11
　Proverbs 13:2–3
　Proverbs 15:1–8
　Proverbs 17:27–28
　Proverbs 18:4–8,12–13,19–21
　Proverbs 16:18–24
　Proverbs 23:9
　Proverbs 27:1–2
　Proverbs 29:11
　Philippians 4:6–8

1 Corinthians 13:1

Chapter Twelve: BASK in the Story
    Proverbs 15:13–15
    Proverbs 1:2–7
    Colossians 3:1–4
    Proverbs 17:22
    Nehemiah 8:10
    1 John 2:20
    Galatians 6:7–10

The author appreciates the references from the New King James Version (NKJV), the New Living Translation (NLT), and the King James Version (KJV) of the Bible.

About the Author

Sid grew up in Grand Island, Nebraska. He was a typical kid, loved the Huskers football team, and dreamed of playing professional basketball. As a student he was a classic underachiever and had four sharp siblings right behind him, "spurring" him on. After high school graduation, he attended a Christian sports camp where he was introduced to a personal relationship with Jesus.

This relationship with Jesus Christ gave the trajectory of Sid's life a dramatic shift upward. Though he still loved sports, he got involved in various Christian ministries and was thrilled by experiencing lives transformed for the better upon hearing the Gospel. He pledged himself to Gospel ministry, and through the influence of godly friends, he became involved in spiritual leadership, seminary, and the local church. He always has been involved in some sort of sports ministry through playing, coaching, or radio.

He married Karen who outclassed him by a mile. Together they have two married children and two grandsons. (Karen works at Compassion International and helps release children from poverty in Jesus' name.) They have enjoyed encouraging each other in life and various ministry adventures. By God's grace, Sid has lived a faithful and fruitful life of faith. He has helped many people through personal evangelism, preaching, counseling, coaching, mentoring, and speaking. He speaks to churches, groups, and on the radio. At present, he is the teaching pastor at Colorado Springs Christian Singles 2, a local outreach and uplifting ministry to singles.

The BASK book series has put fresh wind in his sails and helped him flow in the current of God's grace. This fun and creative series of Bible- teaching books is helping people discover freedom in Christ and a refreshing perspective about the Christian life.

Sid lives to "wear the CROWN" and helps others wear the CROWN, too. He explains the CROWN as Christ, Righteousness, Order, Worship, and Nobility. He draws this inspiration from Isaiah 61:1-3:

1
The Spirit of the Sovereign Lord is on me,
because the Lord has anointed me

to proclaim good news to the poor.
He has sent me to bind up the brokenhearted,
to proclaim freedom for the captives
and release from darkness for the prisoners,
2
to proclaim the year of the Lord's favor
and the day of vengeance of our God,
to comfort all who mourn,
3
and provide for those who grieve in Zion—
to bestow on them a crown of beauty
instead of ashes,
the oil of joy
instead of mourning,
and a garment of praise
instead of a spirit of despair.
They will be called oaks of righteousness,
a planting of the Lord
for the display of his splendor.
(Isaiah 61:1–3)

www.ingramcontent.com/pod-product-compliance
Lightning Source LLC
LaVergne TN
LVHW051547070426
835507LV00021B/2456